BREAKING THROUGH THE CLOUDS

BREAKING THROUGH
THE CLOUDS

Richard F. Fleck

PRUETT PUBLISHING COMPANY
BOULDER, COLORADO

© 2004 by Richard Fleck

All rights reserved. No part of this book may be reproduced without written permission from the publisher, except in the case of brief excerpts in critical reviews and articles. Address all inquiries to: Pruett Publishing Company, PO Box 2140, Boulder, Colorado 80306; www.pruettpublishing.com.

Printed in the United States of America

11 10 09 08 07 06 05 04   5 4 3 2 1

Library of Congress Cataloging-in-Publication Data

Fleck, Richard F., 1937–
  Breaking through the clouds : / Richard F. Fleck.– 1st ed.
    p. cm.
  Includes bibliographical references and index.
  ISBN 0-87108-934-3 (alk. paper)
  1. Mountaineering–West (U.S.) 2. Fleck, Richard F., 1937–
Travel–West (U.S.) I. Title.

  GV199.42.W39F54 2004
  796.52'2'0979–dc22
                                            2004016115

Design & Composition by Dave Consulting

DEDICATION

To my wife, Maura, and my children, Rich, Michelle, and Maureen, with whom I have shared many an alpine hour. And to their spouses and children.

TABLE OF CONTENTS

Acknowledgments ix

Tabeguache Prelude 1

CHAPTER ONE — Early Allure of Longs Peak 5
Including 4 parts on getting ready, night and day climbs, and a hearkening back to Major Powell

CHAPTER TWO — High in the Mummy Range 25
Including 2 parts on winter and summer climbs

CHAPTER THREE — Asian and Alaskan Interludes 33

CHAPTER FOUR — Where Land is Mostly Sky 43
Including 2 parts on Grays and Torreys and Bierstadt

CHAPTER FIVE — 4-Corner High 53
Including 4 parts on Uintas, San Francisco Peaks, Elbert, and Wheeler

CHAPTER SIX — Viva Los Pecos y La Sierra de San Juan 87

CHAPTER SEVEN — A New England Interlude 97

CHAPTER EIGHT — Solace of Dinosaur Ridge 101

CHAPTER NINE — A Close Call on Mount Princeton 109

CHAPTER TEN — Rambles Along the Mosquito Range 115

CHAPTER ELEVEN — Multiple Ascents: Evans and Pikes 125

CHAPTER TWELVE — Mountains Over the Desert 135

A FINALE — Sacred Black Hills 145

Black Elk's Prayer Atop Harney Peak 157

A Selective List Of Formative Mountain And Nature Books ... 159

Index 161

About the Author 165

A Chronological List of Books by Richard F. Fleck 166

ACKNOWLEDGMENTS

"Getting Ready on Mount Katahdin" originally appeared in *Boston Review*.

"Longs Peak by Night" originally appeared in *Appalachia*.

"Hearkening Back to Major Powell's Ascent" originally appeared in *The Climbing Art*.

"High in the Mummy Range," Parts I and II, originally appeared in *Appalachia* and *Colorado Outdoors*, respectively.

"Where Land is Mostly Sky" originally appeared in *The Climbing Art*.

"Unita Unity" and "Viva los Pecos y La Sierra de San Juan" originally appeared in *Where Land Is Mostly Sky* (Passeggiata Press, 1997).

"Ascent to Infinity" originally appeared in *Paintbrush: A Journal of Poetry and Translation*.

"Fuji San: Climbing Among the Stars" originally appeared in *Appalachia*.

"The Snows of Halla San" originally appeared in *Kansai Timeout* (Japan).

The author wishes to acknowledge, with thanks, permission of the Research Library of the New York State Historical Association to publish Black Elk's hitherto unpublished prayer atop a rocky perch on Harney Peak.

TABEGUACHE PRELUDE

Stinging sleet came in waves from ever-darkening clouds to the west. My boots were wet and my knees were wobbly, yet we had to continue down to safety, having climbed the southernmost peak of Colorado's Sawatch Range—Mount Tabeguache. Unconcerned mountain goats grazed peacefully on a grassy ledge a half mile away. Their wet white wool shone in a beam of sunlight that punctured billows of gray clouds.

Just forty-five minutes ago we stood atop Tabeguache Peak. There we nibbled on crackers and oranges and stared into space. To the north were Mounts Antero and Princeton, and across the way to our immediate east was Mount Shavano, gray and bald in an early September sun. We could not see from this vantage point the legendary snowfield in the shape of an angel that lies on Shavano's eastern flank. Legend has it that a young Tabeguache Ute woman prayed for rain during a severe drought and willingly submitted to sacrificing herself toward this goal. Every spring a snowfield appears in the shape of an angel—the angel of Shavano. We continued our gazing southeastward toward the distant and somewhat hazy Sangre de Cristos. A brisk wind buffeted us up there with a temperature in the low forties. We knew that Denver was roasting in the nineties and took some solace in the contrast. More than once we ducked from diving swallows flying precariously close to Tabeguache's summit and our heads. Food and the view energized us. But we worried about an energized sky filled with a fast-approaching thunderstorm.

We gingerly continued our lateral descent across scree and loose rocks covered with brilliant lichens that varied in color from orange to green, and emphasized all the more with splats of rain and sleet. Black clouds raced in from the west. It looked grim, but we steadily descended from Tabeguache's lofty 14,157-foot summit to 13,000 feet, recorded on my son's altimeter. Amazingly, the clouds scattered and the sun poked through as we reached a south-running ridge with camel humps. Each step up one of the humps came with cramps in my legs and knees. We saw bighorn sheep to the west moving along ridges with graceful agility. We paused for water and dried Turkish apricots and noticed clusters of alpine sandworts and elk sedges whose sepals already had begun to turn crimson. From wooded valleys far below came the sound of squeaking, rusty castle gates slowly opening and closing—bull elk bugling to signal the beginning of rutting season.

Last night, in our primitive campsite at 10,500 feet, we had been serenaded by elk mystically bugling from both afar and near. In the tent, I had drifted back to my ranger days in Rocky Mountain National Park when I was stationed at Moraine Park. It was autumn and the first heavy, wet snow had fallen. Mist had risen, phantomlike, from the meadows, and hundreds of elk had bugled in rapid succession. It had seemed like I was on another planet. It had been difficult concentrating on writing accession numbers on museum specimens.

Also in our tent last night beneath the base of Tabeguache, I thought about the tribe for whom this mountain was named.

Shavano was a leader of the Tabeguache Ute tribe and befriended white settlers in these south-central mountains of Colorado. But more and more miners came in search of gold on the flanks of Mounts Tabeguache and Shavano in violation of the Brunot Treaty of 1873 signed by the Utes. Chief Shavano's trip to Washington, D.C. to protest these intrusions a few years later proved fruitless. Eventually, the government forced this mountain tribe of Utes to live in an arid southwestern corner of Colorado near Mesa Verde.

Just before dozing off, I remembered our planning this trip with maps of the Sawatch Range spread out on the table. Tabeguache had stood out at the beginning of this range, flanked by high thirteeners and Mount Shavano. We had chosen to ascend Tabeguache the following Saturday morning in early September.

My son thought he saw a large, four-legged animal through the tent walls the night before our ascent. I remained asleep while he worried whether or not it was a bear or an elk. Apparently, whatever it was, it wandered away harmlessly. We awakened as early as our friend Michael in another tent. We immediately poured coffee and ate breakfast bars as we packed our day sacks for the climb ahead of us.

The morning remained as clear as the previous starlit evening. We found the trail and bounded straight up through an aspen grove all aglow with golden and orange leaves and soon reached a dead-timber zone. Each twisted and nude trunk looked like the kingdom of Oz. But the steepness of the trail forced us back to reality. That trail was no tourist trail—it went straight up with loose gravel and pebbles. We would take two steps ahead and one sliding step backward. It was tiring—very tiring. The flanks of Mount Shavano, however, gradually came into view, as did high thirteeners to our west. The tundra of September had a distinct rust color. We at last reached a fairly level tundra plateau and drank water and gobbled trail mix. White spots on the distant tundra proved to be a flock of mountain goats. We put on fleece jackets in the stiff wind. Clearly, autumn had arrived at this altitude. Just two weeks later I would fly over Mounts Tabeguache and Shavano on a flight from Las Vegas to Denver. They appeared out the aircraft window all white under mounds of fresh snow.

Then we arrived back at this very same spot on our way down. This time we saw up close two bevies of ptarmigan changing from summer to winter plumage with fluffy white feathers underneath. Despite the approaching storm, my son Rich took a close-up shot while Michael and I stared at the birds, their beady eyes staring right back. More black clouds rolled in from the west and gusts of wind pelted us. Though my knees were hardly prepared for the straight-down, loose-gravel trail, I had no other choice but to follow, as best as I could, two agile young men who danced down the trail toward the safety of tree line. Cautious at first, I inched my way down but gradually allowed myself the freedom of sliding in the dust. It was, nonetheless, tiring work. Perhaps fifteen or twenty minutes later I arrived where Rich and Michael sat in dead tree branches awaiting my arrival. It remained chilly even some 2,500 feet lower than the summit.

With wobbly sets of knees we continued our trek down this steep trail into thicker forests of golden aspen. Rain splattered down, making the trail too slick for any rollicking. Each step was taken with utmost care. I could no longer see my young companions ahead. The trail seemed endless. True, there were no longer loose rocks, alpine winds, and sleet pellets, but the trail remained tiresome. I arrived at a little fork in the trail and hoped that I was taking the right one back to the road below. I spotted my son waiting for me at the bottom of the hill, and it felt great to see him. We ambled slowly down the trail and out onto the road, where Michael was changing his boots to more comfortable and softer shoes. We were all thankful to have made this climb, my twenty-fifth of seventeen different 14,000-foot peaks. Tabeguache challenged all three of us, and it pushed me to my physical limits. How could I not but feel a sense of exhilaration despite temporary weariness? In its own way, Mount Tabeguache provided us with something close to a vision quest, showing us throughout the climb our utter dependency on nature as well as our own inner strengths.

CHAPTER ONE

EARLY ALLURE OF LONGS PEAK

Part I — Getting Ready on Mount Katahdin

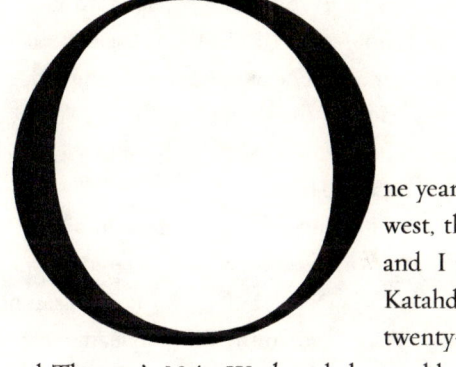

One year prior to coming west, three companions and I climbed Mount Katahdin during my twenty-first birthday. I had read Thoreau's *Maine Woods* and thoroughly delighted in the mysticism of this wild region, with 5,200-foot Mount Katahdin looming above. There was no better place to listen to the piercing voice of the white-throated sparrow from high atop a pagodalike white pine or the eerie cry of the loon on the waters of Moosehead Lake. In Maine, it was not difficult to imagine the ghost of Henry David Thoreau seen faintly through the flickering flames of a campfire.

We camped at Chimney Pond before our first ascent of Mount Katahdin. It was late August, and the nighttime sky throbbed with colored threads of the northern lights. We had difficulty closing our eyes to get some sleep. Yet seemingly, only moments later, we were rolling up our sleeping bags all covered with hoarfrost at 5 a.m. and, like French Jesuits of old, were following a trail through thick black spruce. The high-rising, exposed granite of Baxter Peak loomed above us; if our eyes focused correctly, we thought we saw a skein of fresh snow on the summit. The spruce and aspen around us seemed utterly still and silent.

Before long we had worked our way through Katahdin's timberline of matted dwarf spruce; sometimes we sank up to our knees trying to get through it, and our boots got soaked in icy rivulets of spring water that trickled under the dense matting. With each ten or fifteen feet gained, we could see more and more of the boreal forests of northern Maine, giving off an aroma that was like incense from some Buddhist temple in Kyoto or Nara. And when our feet touched nothing but naked granite, we began to see distant Moosehead Lake and cow-moose-shaped Mount Kineo, mythologized by the Penobscot Indians. We paused to take a few swallows of icy spring water gushing out of a crevice; the sudden chill made our teeth hurt. Although the sky was bright and sunny, a chill wind drilled through us up here, 4,000 feet above the relatively flat terrain surrounding Katahdin's base.

Finally we stood on the rugged and spiny summit of Mount Katahdin, more than 5,000 feet high, and peered down sheer granite cliffs into the glacial cirque of Chimney Pond. Scanning the far horizon, we could clearly discern the distant gleaming thread of the Saint Lawrence River. We hadn't expected to see such sweeping alpine terrain east of the Mississippi, but wild and sweeping it was! As clouds gathered and poured over Katahdin's Knife Edge Ridge to the east, the temperature dropped twenty degrees, helping preserve the tiny crests of fresh snow between the rocks. Dense clouds seemed to be born at our very feet. We elected to descend. Thoreau, a hundred years earlier, called this rocky perch an unfinished part of the globe that robbed him of his "divine faculties." In a sense, all of us standing there could have agreed with him in that the flood of sensations was too quick, too vast, to be absorbed in a reasonable period of time. This one-day climb entered the core of my spirit in undecipherable ways and prepared me well for the coming summer

2,000 miles away in the Rocky Mountains of Colorado, where a seasonal ranger job awaited me.

Part II -- Longs Peak by Night

One summer night when I worked as a ranger at Milner Pass, I mused about the highest point of land in Rocky Mountain National Park. I had climbed Mount Ida and Specimen Mountain earlier, but now I was to climb Longs Peak with three other rangers, including long-time friend Robert Barbee (former superintendent of Yellowstone National Park during the fires of 1988). In preparation for what was to be a midnight climb, I read Isabella Bird's *A Lady's Life in the Rocky Mountains*. There could be no better place to read this book than my cabin in the sky, surrounded by a spruce forest that was illuminated by moonbeams two miles above sea level. Isabella Bird prepared me well by opening my mind and spirit to the mystical glories of 14,000 feet, my first of many such peaks.

The Utes were the first to climb Longs Peak well before white man deemed it possible; they went up there to trap eagles for war feathers. Major Stephen H. Long, who conducted an exploratory expedition to the Rocky Mountains in 1820, is credited with the first written description of this block-shaped mountain—hence its name. Major John Wesley Powell, a one-armed Civil War hero and author of *The Exploration of the Colorado River and its Canyons*, successfully led a climbing expedition in 1868 to the 14,255-foot summit. As if his ascent wasn't enough, the following summer Major Powell and his men braved the rapids of the Colorado River from Green River, Wyoming, to the Grand Wash beyond the Grand Canyon of Arizona. Ten years after Powell's ascent of Longs Peak, an Englishwoman by the name of Isabella Bird became the second lady ever to climb the mountain. Her description in the aforementioned book of the lower valleys and mountain views from this highest northernmost peak of the Front Range is both poetic and artistic:

From this we ascended into the purple gloom of great forests which clothe the skirts of the mountains up to a height of about 11,000 feet, and from these chill and solitary depths we had glimpses of golden atmosphere and rose-lit summits, not of the land very far off, but of the land nearer now in all its grandeur, gaining in sublimity by nearness—glimpses, too, through a broken vista of purple gorges, of the illimitable plains lying idealized in late summer, their baked, brown expanse transfigured into the likeness of a sunset sea rilling infinitely in a wave of misty gold.

Higher up, her climb turned into something different—she was tugged nearly all the way from the 12,000-foot-high boulder field to the summit by a man called Mountain Jim. She wrote:

The intense dryness of the day and the rarefaction of the air, at a height of nearly 15,000 feet, made respiration very painful. There is always water on the peak, but it was frozen hard as rock, and the sucking of ice and snow increases thirst. We all suffered severely from want of water, and the gasping for breath made our mouths and tongues so dry that articulation was difficult, and the speech of all unnatural.

How strange it must have been for Isabella Bird, a Victorian lady, to be standing atop lumpy, frozen ground so far removed from the valleys of comfort below.

Our turn came for Longs Peak. Stars shone with absolute brilliance as I drove across Trail Ridge Road to meet Bob Barbee, Dick DeLong, and Jim Jewell. We signed the register at 10 o'clock p.m. to begin a spectacular nighttime ascent of the peak that Arapaho Indians call *Nestoaíeux* (two guides). Our plan—to arrive at the boulder field by midnight, the cables above 13,000 feet by 3 a.m., and the summit itself just before sunrise. As at Mount Katahdin's base two years ago, we would experience the pulsing threads of northern lights, only this time we'd be right up there in the living sky itself. And on that night we would witness a total eclipse of the moon.

Plodding along the trail, we wound our way through lodgepole pines toward the summit eight miles distant. At first our breathing seemed heavy, and the quiet night air accentuated our human sounds. As our lungs gradually accustomed themselves to the task, however, we commenced a four-way conversation that had the uncanny effect of disrupting natural silence. Our voices sounded quite out of place in that still alpine air. Soon we ceased talking and kept our thoughts to ourselves. Only when we stopped to rest did we realize how frigid this July evening air was. In such chilly air, the very sound of an ice-cold brook tumbling over dark rocks made me shiver. Four miles deeper into the forest, we paused by an iridescent stream to fill our canteens and put on some warmer clothing. Stars peppered the black dome above us. It felt good to be a part of a community of climbers, rather than lonely on a solitary climb. We proceeded onward with a golden moon rising through creaking branches of spruce and fir. John Muir once described such creaking as a kind of forest violin. Five hundred more vertical feet and tree line!

The trail leveled out a bit, allowing us to proceed at an easier pace until we reached the boulder field at 12,600 feet. This is where the walk ends and the climb begins, as Isabella Bird discovered. The moon illuminated numerous scrubby evergreens growing here and there under the icy masses on Mount Meeker (13,911 feet) and Longs Peak. Gnarled, twisted limber pines, crinkly monument plants, and dwarf willows looked extraterrestrial. At the upper end of the boulder field, we all caught sight of the fairy-blinking array of the city lights of Denver some 7,000 feet lower. We stood amid the true alpine tundra zone, with its delicate mosses and flowers barely visible in the black shadows of the mountains. Slithering over loose rocks like crustaceans at the bottom of an immense lagoon, we inched our way up Longs Peak flanked by horizontal strips of white snow.

As we rested on a huge boulder, we nervously chatted about an upcoming event—the total eclipse of the moon, our only sufficient source of light. The eclipse would occur around 3 a.m., and we knew it would take longer than two hours to complete our ascent. We hoped to get past the tricky hundred yards or so of cable (no longer in existence) that aid climbers over a very sheer part of the north face. On went our gloves, as we plodded toward Chasm View, some 13,200 feet high. At this altitude, breathing can be a bit of a problem;

our minds became drowsy and our feet just did not seem to function properly. It seemed as if sheer desire rather than physical power pushed us on toward Chasm View.

We all had slight headaches when we sat down on overhanging ledges at Chasm View. We stared in wonderment at the awesome heights of the famed Diamond Face rising above and the black waters of Chasm Lake 2,000 feet below. Surely such a place manifests what John Muir meant by the spiritual magnetism of mountains. Despite weariness of body, the spirit seems to ramble out into the cosmos of granite, stars, and moon.

We remained in a trance until Jim Jewell suggested we climb on toward the summit. Just as we were about to arrive at the point where the cable begins, the moon slowly disappeared. Now, only the stars glimmered above a dark frame of cold rock. Suddenly I shouted, "Look to the north!" Way up toward the Wyoming line, pulsing low in the sky, threads of northern lights began to shimmer; it seemed strange that we had to look *down* at them through crags and notches of dark cliff. Were we on the moon itself? Is that why it disappeared?

We missed the cable. In spite of searching for what seemed an eternity in pitch blackness (save for the dim glimmer of fading northern lights and our inadequate flashlights), we failed to find our iron guide. Worming our way up a narrow chimney in the cliff, we struggled to reach a ledge for a rest. Lo and behold, the cable! The four of us unfortunately had taken the most difficult route to the cable's beginning, shining so dimly in the granite overhead. Each of us grabbed the cable, took steps, and pulled upward, sluggishly repeating the process many times, like brutes in slow motion. Reaching the top of the cable, we crossed some slippery, crusted ice at a snail's pace that tired us to our limits. The moon slowly reappeared. Oh, for a warm sleeping bag to curl up in and the time to doze for a half century.

Attaining an altitude of about 14,000 feet, we had to rest just one more time before reaching the summit itself. The town lights in the warm July prairie far below seemed unreal. A rosy finch flicked past our heads to draw us out of our trance. Bob Barbee shouted, "Two hundred feet to go!" Up we stood, forcing our weary bones to move, until we rambled out onto the small peneplain summit of Longs Peak. It wasn't difficult to imagine a weary Isabella Bird gasping for breath and being comforted by Mountain Jim.

Since neither food nor drink appealed to us so much as sleep, we stretched out on flat boulders. But only fifteen minutes passed before the chattering of our own teeth awakened us. By this time, a faint reddish hue was becoming visible in the frosty air. The dull-green, lake-studded prairie gradually assumed a more realistic appearance. As the sun bobbed up over the rim of the earth, we all squinted like blind bats at midday. The whole Front Range glowed in a golden light, while the narrow valleys far below remained dim and gray. We felt like Ute warriors standing there, arms folded, staring out at the space of snowfield and mountain in the crisp morning air. The distant Never Summer Range glowed in the rising sun; my mind drifted back to the previous summer when I had the good fortune of watching a high Never Summer flock of bighorn ewes taking turns guarding their lambs. Up here on the summit of Longs Peak, something began to happen—the Brocken Specter (to which John Muir refers in *The Mountains of California*). The vast, block-shaped shadow of Longs Peak spread and stretched westward some sixty miles as our Earth planet rotated. We stood in absolute silence. Only once more in my life would I witness such a phenomenon—on top of Mount Fuji in Japan.

The descent to the boulder field proved rewarding. Each foot of granite varied as would Pennsylvania Dutch farm country from the air—a patchwork of vegetational designs. Orange, yellow, black, and green crusty lichens with dense patches of Irish-green moss and brownish-black liverwort encrusted the cliff sides all the way down to Chasm View. The charm of this color scheme overpowered the tired pain of our legs and feet and gave us something to muse on all the way down to the comfort of the valleys below.

PART III — LONGS PEAK BY DAY

Permit me to digress to my first impressions of this mountain. One's initial view of Longs Peak from Estes Park is simply waylaying.

The beholder sees it rising up into a fringe of cloud with its diamond face of granite like a giant commanding respect from all in the wooded vales or on the sparkling lakes below. The peak never quite left my mind all during ranger training at Rocky Mountain National Park. Although my duty was to lead small groups of people up Specimen Mountain on the park's west side, every time we reached the summit and looked across at distant and much higher Longs Peak, I knew I must sometime climb the king of Colorado's northern Rockies. But this opportunity did not come until the following summer, when I and a fellow ranger used one of our days off to attempt both Longs Peak and its nearby companion, Mount Meeker, some 300 feet lower.

We arose early on a crisp morning in early July and soon found ourselves walking up the trail above Longs Peak Campground, delighting in the fragrance of the dense lodgepole pine forest. Canada jays squawked and magpies fluttered from branch to branch. A roaring stream tumbled out of Chasm Lake, still several thousand feet above.

Raisins and water replenished our youthful energy until we reached the boulder field at the base of a sheer wall of granite rising skyward. I gazed to the west to see Flattop Mountain. Last summer we crossed Flattop, taking the seventeen-mile trek up over the tundra to Grand Lake. I remember descending into the lusher forests of the Western Slope and being reminded of the Maine woods. We carefully descended the rocks beside Wardance Falls and rambled over to Lake Nanita, the Walden of the Rockies. Hummingbirds buzzed from clusters of purple monkshood up to the nests to feed the chicks. A bull elk crashed through young aspen, knocking over a tree as though it were a mere clothes pole. We gathered dark purple grouseberries in the woods outside of Grand Lake Village and had a soda jerk make grouseberry sundaes for all of us.

But now we faced the boulder field. We slowly trudged up to Chasm View to peer 2,000 feet downward at iceberg-riddled Chasm Lake. I had to inch backward a bit, as the depths below gave me vertigo. My partner and I carefully climbed up the cable route, where we appreciated the assistance over the most sheer part of the north face. From atop the cables we climbed gingerly across loose scree up to the flat summit of Longs Peak, a process so much easier than during our nighttime climb.

Seeing thunderheads build up to the west, we immediately descended the south face of the peak via the Keplinger Couloir and angled toward Mount Meeker. We thought we had descended far enough to easily cross over and climb to the top of Meeker, but no, we traversed ever so slowly across to the top of the notch and stared down into several hundred feet of space separating the two peaks that the Arapahos called *Nestoaieux*. We didn't dare proceed any farther and slowly inched our way back up to the summit of Longs Peak. Thirteen years later, three of us used all of our energy to arrive at the summit and hardly even thought of crossing over to Mount Meeker—the difference between being twenty-two and thirty-five! This time we elected to descend, not the cable route, but the Keyhole route around the back side of Longs Peak. We followed the painted circles on the rock that guided us down through chutes and chimneys to the western side of the peak that sported jagged spires touching the sky. One of these spires had a hole in it! We passed through the keyhole and down to the familiar boulder field, then followed the trail back to Longs Peak Campground. We glanced back at massive Longs Peak, first climbed by Major John Wesley Powell and company in 1868. They came across from Grand Lake via the North Inlet and Flattop Mountain and McHenry's Peak, descended to Wild Basin and Sandbeach Lake, camped, and ascended the summit via the Keplinger Couloir up the south side of the peak on August 23, 1868. Nothing like adding seventeen miles to your climb all the way from Grand Lake!

PART IV — A Hearkening Back to Major Powell's Ascent*

Major John Wesley Powell and his men regrouped along the shores of deep, blue Grand Lake at the headwaters of the Grand River

---

* Information for my historic narrative came from Donald Worster's *River Running West: A Life of John Wesley Powell* (Oxford University Press, 2001, pp. 147–149), which pinpoints their route.

(later known as the Colorado River) on a very fine day of August 20, 1868. Powell had been fortunate enough to obtain modest support for an exploring party along the headwaters of the Grand River by the United States Congress, which appropriated monies for rations, and by Illinois college students, who agreed to pay expense monies to come along and collect specimens for museums back home. During the next summer, ten of them would explore, with cedar boats, the length of the Colorado River from Green River, Wyoming, to the Grand Wash on the western side of Arizona's Grand Canyon. Happily, his men, including his brother Walter, Lewis Keplinger, Samuel Garman, William Byers (of *The Rocky Mountain News*), and two local boys, Jack Sumner and Ned Farrell, agreed to climb Longs Peak. The mountain was a great symbol of the beginning of the Grand River, which flowed into the Green River in Utah to become the mighty Colorado River, which, in turn, carved its way to the Sea of Cortez. What a journey from 14,250-odd feet down to sea level in 1,500 miles! Certainly they must have had a tremendous campfire the night before their climb. Their campfire reflected off the waters of Grand Lake as sparks danced skyward to meet the stars. The sky—the Big Dipper, Jupiter, and Mars—held their attention beyond sleeping hours. There was even the faintest trace of a shimmering, faint-green aurora borealis. Powell hardly noticed the pain in the stump of his arm, amputated after the Battle of Shiloh only a few years earlier.

A hearty breakfast of fresh trout and fire-roasted potatoes more than prepared them for their first day's hike, as they followed the North Inlet through dense forests of lodgepole pine. At a higher elevation, spruce and fir sweetly perfumed the air. Their packs contained rations for more than a week. Their pack mules toted bacon, flour, water, a Dutch oven, bedrolls, and some scientific equipment. Much to Powell's pleasure, Keplinger, an eager college lad, led the way.

It is not difficult to imagine that they must have observed such things as a small and delicate nest with three tiny beaks protruding skyward, awaiting a mother hummingbird that was buzzing her wings just beyond reach of their beaks. They would have marveled at the mother as she pushed her beak into their wide-open mouths to give each of them a dose of mountain nectar. Such clear, azure-blue skies they had never seen before. The American West was great, thought Major Powell, for more than its wealth of minerals! Each breath of air restored a wholeness to body and spirit.

Their way grew steeper and the air much thinner. Up there the trees appeared stunted and twisted by winter winds, yet they possessed a sublimity of their own. Garman, their Quaker companion, reflected on the peacefulness of the scene. If only humans could live in such peace, he remarked. Having suffered the wounds of the War between the States, how could Major Powell not agree? They paused to take a drink of icy stream water, so cold it made their teeth hurt. They all took out some hardtack and jerky to make a light lunch for themselves as they listened to the splash of waterfalls tumbling down from mountain snow. They rested on rocks coated with orange lichen and tan, fleshy liverwort. Indians said that one could survive on liverwort if no other food was available.

A crashing and crackling of rocks sliding off some ledge above startled all of them, including their pack mules with bulging eyes. The rocks fell through space, as if in slow motion, thumping harmlessly into a subalpine marsh lush with glacier lilies. They all stood in a trance, but soon Powell advised his men to push onward and upward. Ideally, they should camp above tree line along a lake's shoreline, if possible, where they could catch trout for dinner and breakfast by means of hand lines. Just as they emerged from the forests, a giant bull elk came running through the valley, crashing into young trees and knocking them over. Was a mountain lion in pursuit? They could only guess.

One can imagine Major Powell's words: "Let's climb just a little higher. Let's find a nice lake above tree line and build a campfire there. I want each of you to carry as many broken branches as possible for firewood."

After some tramping, they spied a small lake that the men later named in the major's honor. It lay beneath the steep tundra slopes of a high peak graced with bands of mist. They selected a camping spot, dumped their collected firewood into a nice pile, and soon had a roaring fire. The two Powell brothers and the Quaker walked over to the lake to fish with hand lines baited with baby grasshoppers collected the day before in a lower, grassy valley. After an hour or so in the dying rays of the sun, all three of them had nibbles on their lines and at last yanked in five or six fine fingerling trout. They ambled back to camp, proud of a string of fish.

"So, what was it like fighting in the Civil War, Major and Captain Powell?" asked the Quaker student.

"I'd rather not talk about it at all," said Powell's brother, Walter.

"We fulfilled our obligation," said the major very quietly, "and, while it was extremely frightening and terrible with men suffering and dying all around, it's something that had to be done. But I agree with my brother, let's not talk about it, especially under these magnificent clear skies of Colorado!"

Powell tried to protect his poor brother from the devastating memories that caused him such emotional suffering. The major offered Walter a pipe filled with tobacco fresh out of his pouch to soothe and calm him. "Yes, will you look at those stars, Walter." When he at last puffed on the pipe and sang a little tune to himself, Powell walked over to Garman, the Quaker, and asked him why he would ask such a foolish question, especially coming from a peace-loving Quaker.

"I didn't mean it that way. I meant to draw out of you two some of your heroic deeds, but I see now that I made a mistake. I'm sorry."

After dinner, a cool breeze chilled them to the bone. They all went over to the pack mules to get bedrolls for some sound sleep before a steep ascent to the tundra the next morning.

A glorious sunrise shone into their faces, awakening them out of their slumber. The mules chomped on lush grasses as the major quickly prepared a fire, put on coffee, and baked some sourdough biscuits in a Dutch oven that was being carried by the pack animals. With a tin mug of coffee in hand, he examined the steep slope they had in store after breakfast. He spotted several bighorn sheep slowly ambling in the lush tundra far above. A marsh hawk sailed overhead in pursuit of his breakfast, no doubt. The men all seemed eager to climb up into the sky to gain their first view of Longs Peak. Rather than taking the pack animals any higher, Powell suggested that his men build a corral of fallen logs in the forests directly below the lake.

Shortly after securing the mules, they shouldered their packs loaded with sleeping gear and hardtack biscuits and water. The major even placed a small bottle of wine in one of his pack's compartments. At first, it was hard going. There was no trail, of course, and blazing their way through soft grasses and entwining dwarf willows proved difficult. Thistle plants turned their heads toward the early morning sun. Pikas and marmots peeped and squeaked in the still air. They could just see over a western ridge into the vast expanse of Grand Lake and the distant Gore Range. They all marveled at the graceful little penny-sized alpine forget-me-nots carpeting the tundra at their feet. They had the most delicate aroma. And here and there, all across the slope, golden sunflowers bloomed like miniature versions of those planted by Mormons across the plains states.

All they could see was a vast sky above the last bit of ridge. They stood, within minutes, atop an unnamed peak, looking across a vast abyss of space to McHenry's Peak and a distant, molar-shaped Longs Peak darkening in summer storm clouds. Powell's men embarrassed him by naming this peak upon which they stood "Powell Peak." Why not leave them be, thought the major, with their Indian names.

Jagged lightning bolts forked the eastern skies about twenty miles away. Moments later, thunder boomed and rumbled and boomed again in this thin alpine air. Powell thought to himself that thunder in Illinois couldn't begin to compare with thunder out here. They sat in a circle and ate some biscuits laced with bacon slabs and heartily drank water out of their canteens. A marmot came begging for food, but they were all too hungry to share any of it with him.

"Well, lads, see yonder peak--McHenry's Peak--let's follow the contour of the terrain over to it and see if we can get across to Longs Peak."

They put on their packs, strapped on canteens, and trekked across incredibly soft and spongy tundra. They clipped along at a fast pace, and within forty-five minutes, they stood atop McHenry's Peak. From there they could see across the valley filled with moraines all the way to the Mummy Range and the distant high plains of Laramie, with its recently completed Union Pacific Railroad. As soon as the transcontinental line was connected in Utah, they would ship cedar boats from Chicago to Green River, Wyoming, to begin another voyage of discovery.

"Hey, my friends," shouted Jack Sumner, "there appears to be a narrow ridge of rock connecting our peak with Longs. Look slightly downhill and eastward!"

"Right you are," said the major.

They immediately hopped down to this narrow, somewhat frightening ridge, and picked their way slowly and carefully across it, trying not to look down 2,000 feet on either side, as the ridge was only a foot and a half wide in places. Distant thunder rumbled as the storm slid harmlessly eastward. Powell's companions used both arms to balance themselves in the wind—a difficult feat for the major, who had only one arm. Wind gusts became dangerous. Major Powell feared that one of them might slip. Only slowly did they approach Chief's Head Peak, sticking up in the sky. Suddenly, Jack Sumner froze with shaken nerves; he couldn't move an inch farther. Keplinger carefully edged passed him. He then encouraged Sumner to continue onward with success. Longs Peak remained illusive and far away. Reaching the summit of Chief's Head, they realized their mistake. There was nothing but gaping space across to Longs Peak. Small alpine birds flicked past their heads, paying no heed to the depths below.

"I have an idea," said the major. "Let's descend into the basin below McHenry's Peak. Look at all those nice lakes below in the valley. Let's descend with care and set up camp on the south side of Longs Peak, then try to climb it from there. Apparently, there's no way to get over to its west-facing or north-facing cliffs."

"I agree," said Keplinger. "Perhaps there is an accessible route up the south side of Longs."

The six men proceeded ever so slowly down a flank of Chief's Head into this southern basin (now called Wild Basin) and breathed sighs of relief when their feet touched flower-clad tundra instead of loose, wobbly rocks. Powell sat down, or rather fell down, in the soft tundra grass near a spot of August snow and admired the bright yellow buttercups growing right out of the snow. Here was spring in the midst of early fall. Probably this patch of tundra would never experience summer before the first snowfall. As they tramped lower toward tree line, they brushed past pink elephantheads and marsh marigolds growing along streamside. Warm bands of valley air rose to greet them after their chilly alpine ramble.

Angling down toward Snowbank Lake, William Byers twisted his ankle on a protruding root. Thankfully, after they bound it with cloth, he was able to walk, very gingerly, along the shoreline. It proved to be only a very slight sprain. They rested a bit before descending even farther down to Sandbeach Lake, which was within direct line of Longs Peak's southern flanks. Here they would camp for the night before attempting to summit Longs Peak, rising some 3,000 feet above. Powell felt at home at Sandbeach Lake, with its thin stand of timber and subalpine fields of purple monkshood and bright blue *Mertensia*, or chiming bells. They set up camp only several miles east as the crow flies of their previous night's camp spot—just a rocky ridge of McHenry's Peak separated them from their pack mules. The evening before their final ascent became quite chilly, making it difficult to fish with such numb fingers, but fish they did and with success—four nice cutthroat trout. Just before pitch darkness, they feasted on fire-roasted trout, sourdough biscuits, and fresh-perked coffee, topped off with a surprise from Keplinger—a tin of juicy peaches from the depths of his pack. Stars peppered the sky, with the Milky Way, or Way of Souls, spread across the inner dome of heaven. The sweet scent of a resinous pine-stick fire made them sleepy in the warmth and comfort of their bedrolls. But another rock slide awakened them late that evening. It seemed to come from the upper flanks of Longs Peak and fell into the soft tundra above them. The major hoped this would not prove to be some sort of omen.

At the slightest hint of daybreak, they awakened one by one. Sumner built up a breakfast fire and put on the coffee. Each of them stuck a wooden stake into thick bacon slabs and cooked them to crispness. Eating and drinking done, they prepared themselves for an exploratory climb to the base of the peak via a delightful small alpine lake that they named in Keplinger's honor, because he had led the way across yesterday's knife-edge ridge. Little rivulets of melting snow trickled into this lake, feeding the roots of marsh marigolds as golden as the rising sun. A stream tumbled out of the south end of Lake Keplinger, making a pleasant gurgling sound in an otherwise very silent alpine theatre. Noticing something bobbing in and out of the outlet stream, Powell walked down a steep hill fifty vertical feet. To his delight and surprise, the bobbing action proved to be that of a water ouzel, or dipper bird, in search of underwater prey.

"Major, what are you doing down there? It's *up* we want to go!" shouted Keplinger.

"A water ouzel caught my eye!"

Keplinger, proud of his knife-edge bravery, proposed that he lead the way up, because he thought he saw the perfect route up the south face—a sort of narrow couloir. The rest of them slowly followed his lead, but some of them, including Powell himself, began to feel the effects of prolonged high altitude, or perhaps the bacon hadn't properly settled in his stomach. Keplinger climbed so quickly that he finally completely disappeared from view. The major worried about his decision. What if he ran into trouble 500 feet above? However, not being able to do much else, he and his men trudged ever so carefully higher and higher until they stood on a ledge affording them a view of Chief's Head directly across a dizzy abyss. Orange and gray lichens coated almost every rock. Green and gleaming mosses dripped with icy water. Powell looked above to see Keplinger coming back down the cliff.

"Major," he shouted, "it's far too steep and scary up there!"

"How close were you to the summit?"

"I'm not sure, but probably within 800 feet."

"Well, Keplinger, I suggest we all get up to that very point in the couloir, and surely all of our sets of eyes will spot a more encouraging route up the last bit of cliff."

"I need to rest, Major Powell. I feel a little shaky."

When he returned back down to their level, they all sat in comfortable positions on a ledge to the left of the couloir. It had become mid-morning, and already they heard very distant rumbles of thunder. Yet the sky above was cobalt blue. A distant raven floated on thermal layers of air and let out with a deep, raucous squawk. Hawks, higher up, perhaps redtails, circled to the east over Mount Meeker. Perhaps they spotted a dead animal of some sort.

"Are you rested, Mr. Keplinger?"

"I suppose so, Major Powell."

"Then, let's go."

They climbed the couloir slowly but steadily as they looked down on the distant Indian Peaks to the south. The couloir narrowed down to a mere chute. This very location proved to be Keplinger's high point.

"Let's proceed up the chute using our shoulders for friction," Powell suggested.

"But Major Powell, what if the chute peters out with nothing but an overhang?" asked Keplinger.

"We'll deal with that when we get there!"

Except for scraping his stump ever so slightly, causing a toothachelike pain, the major managed to negotiate the chute well. Others both behind and ahead of him kept on plodding upward as though heaven itself were their destination. More thunder, this time a little closer! Powell could not help but notice a dark patch of cloud to the west. Keplinger once again disappeared from view. What is that man doing? Then three others disappeared! Finally Powell disappeared from view of William Byers below. Why? They stood on the summit! Soon, all six of them gathered together up there on a small peneplain covered with dark slabs of frozen rock. A chilly breeze, too chilly for their thin garb, numbed them to the bone. Powell carefully removed a barometer from his pack and took a measurement. There they stood on August 23, 1868, on the summit of Longs Peak at 14,255 feet above the level of the sea and some 6,000 feet above Grand Lake and the winding Grand River. The view? Unbelievable! Kansas stretched eastward. A vast array of the Rocky Mountain chain loomed to the north. They could clearly discern the distant, very white Medicine Bow Mountains of southern Wyoming. Their cedar boats would travel by rail in just nine months around those mountains to Green River City. To their south, they could see very clearly Pikes Peak and all the rugged mountains in-between! To their west, they looked down on Chief's Head, McHenry's Peak, and the more distant and appropriately named Never Summer Range. Beyond this range, they could see the great Colorado Plateau stretching westward toward Utah. They felt like Ute warriors up there on the roof of the world, with the high point of the Grand River flowing southwesterly to become *El Río Colorado*. Immediately below them lay the sublimely picturesque valley of Estes Park, with its shining glacial knobs and dense forests. Powell's spirit seemed to soar like a hawk so high above the valleys and plains.

"Well, don't just stand there and stare, you fellas," said Keplinger. "Sign your names on this sheet of paper! When you're finished, I'll put the document inside this old baking soda tin, and we'll place it under a rock so men of the future will know that this is the first recorded ascent of the great sentinel of the plains—Longs Peak!"

Mr. Byers, though quite weary, took out his notepad and pencil and started jotting down his thoughts for a *Rocky Mountain News* article. Then Powell brought out his surprise bottle of wine and christened their mountain register. He offered all a sip, except for the Quaker, who shunned such extravagance and even warned Mr. Byers not to include his name as one who indulged in wine. They all stared at each other, wondering if they actually stood up here in the heavens. Powell was so proud of his men. They could have easily refused to make this climb by lingering along the pleasant shores of Grand Lake so far below. Thunder boomed, this time even closer, and they made a quick descent of the narrow chute leading to what became known henceforth as Keplinger's Couloir.

Approaching the lower end of the couloir, the major felt just a bit dizzy, but his happiness overruled. Pipits flicked past their heads as they hopped down to the bottom of the wider couloir, and within an hour or so they trekked across tundra back to Snowbank Lake. Keplinger and Garman wanted to take some further measurements atop McHenry's Peak. Powell told them firmly to watch for sudden storms. The rest of them took the easier route across soft and green tundra, down to gleaming Lake Powell and their corralled pack mules. They caught and roasted cutthroat trout, which peeled right off the bone and into their mouths.

"Well, my lads, what do you think of yourselves now that you've climbed to the highest point above the headwaters of the Grand River?"

"We're almost too tired to think at all."

"Into your bedrolls, men, and sleep well."

"I hope Keplinger and Garman are safe up there on McHenry's Peak," said Sumner.

"Oh, they'll be quite alright. We'll see them in a day or two back at Grand Lake," said the major.

He couldn't sleep at all until, perhaps, the wee hours of the morning. He kept thinking about that view atop Longs Peak. He couldn't bear waiting nine months to get into their white cedar boats that were being built in Chicago. The major could see in his mind's eye Green River City, Wyoming, far out in the rolling sagebrush desert. He could even hear the train whistle piercing the still air as it pushed away from them toward Utah, while they shoved off a small island in the stream and began their river run into the great unknown.

CHAPTER TWO

HIGH IN THE MUMMY RANGE

Part I — Mount Chapin

For Thanksgiving holiday, a group of us from the Colorado State University Outing Club boarded my old jalopy and several other cars to drive across bright red hogbacks covered with damp, gray sagebrush. We wound our way from Fort Collins by back roads toward Big Thompson Canyon. Five of us would climb a mountain while the rest prepared a Thanksgiving supper at a friend's cabin. Rolling mile-high prairie spread below us, purple with haze and dotted with bright lakes and ponds in a gleaming sun. Aged and leafless cottonwoods fingered their way across the sunny prairie. We entered a dark canyon with granite cliffs rising hundreds of feet to meet the sun, creating a haiku of contrast. By now, any inner stagnation of the mind had dissipated. Jack pines clung here and there on the layered canyon walls, scenting the air. The roar of the cascades of the Big Thompson River intensified as the river rounded the Pillar of Hercules, a sheer, eighty-foot rock face rising out of tumbling white water and marking the entrance to Big Thompson Canyon. All we could think of was making a winter ascent of 12,454-foot Mount Chapin in Rocky Mountain National Park just ahead.

We turned off the Big Thompson road onto the Devil's Gulch Canyon road, where scaly-barked Douglas fir and red ponderosa pine swayed and creaked with late autumn breezes. As we continually gained altitude, that balmy, late Indian summer air of the prairie gave way to the chilling winds that were racing down from the high country. In a somewhat protected hollow, a few aspen trees, still with withered leaves, trembled. Twisting our way up the dusty switchbacks, we couldn't help but notice how stark all the aspens, willows, and cottonwoods had become. We at last gained a view of the broad, open valley of Estes Park, glistening with sparkling snow. The whole Mummy Range spread before us, including Mounts Chapin, Chiquita, Epsilon, Fairchild, Hagues, and commanding Mummy Mountain (13,425 feet). What a perfect day for a climb under skies of azure!

Driving past scores of mule deer, elk, and several trotting coyotes in Horseshoe Park, we continued on our last motorized lap up several hairpin turns on the old Fall River Road, some thirty-five years after my grandparents had driven it in a Model T all the way from Philadelphia past walls of snow leading up to Fall River Pass. They wrote across the top of their photos, "Summer Snow!" We put on our packs and gear at Chasm Falls, anticipating *winter* snow.

Our ten feet commenced a slow but steady pace over crackling, dead bracken ferns and through a dense lodgepole pine forest. We hoped to reach the shoulder of a ridge that led to tree line at the base of the peak. The extreme steepness of the trail and the weight of our winter gear tired us quickly, since we were not yet acclimated to the 10,000-foot elevation. Climbing over logs, dried Canada thistle, and crusty patches of snow, we continually gained altitude, noting that the lodgepole pines had yielded to dense stands of incredibly tall Englemann spruce and subalpine fir. When we, at last, reached a windswept shoulder of Chapin, the temperature dropped by twenty degrees. The whole panorama of landscapes through which we had traveled spread before us. The wind, however, made it quite difficult for us to maintain a hold on hard-packed ice.

After a mile or so of plodding through foot-deep snow, we found a rocky promontory where we warmed up with hot soup, bread, and coffee. The usual Canada jays hopped around, begging for food. Their squawking attracted smaller but hardy winter residents—gray and black chickadees. This brief rest with food gave us the energy necessary to forge on toward the summit. The comforting squeak of chickaree squirrels gradually faded as we entered tree line at 11,500 feet. Squat and twisted limber pines hissed in the ever-howling wind. It had become cold enough to make us shiver if we did not keep moving. There was no bare ground—just frozen, icy snow. Blasting gusts of acid-stinging wind howled above matted groves of dwarfed spruce, warning us of what was to come. No longer would we have the shelter of a warm forest. The temperature hovered around zero, with screaming wind sounding somewhat like the South Col of Everest. Breathing became difficult at 12,000 feet, and I felt such a fatigue as I had never experienced during my summertime climbs.

But our weariness soon abated. There, as we edged our way around a stony knoll, six bighorn rams walked gracefully on frozen alpine terrain as though they were taking a stroll in Central Park. As we stared at these creatures, storm clouds began to gather. We moved on toward the summit across treacherous ice. The sheep, however, obviously thought it to be child's play. They continued to amble along, unconcerned with us or the ice. Our summit loomed above us by only several hundred feet, but the ice harassed us every inch of the way. After fifty feet or so, we came to the base of a hard-packed snowfield encrusting the mountain's crest as far as we could see. Out came our ice axes, and slowly we began carving steps up the steep white slope.

When I reached the halfway point, I stopped to rest and look out into the heart of the high country. My sense of novelty at being in such a precarious position in howling wind changed to trepidation. Like a starfish, I clung tightly and slithered my way up until I reached the summit. There the wind proved powerful enough to flatten me. All five of us stood hypnotized by sheer open space. To the south lay the ice-blanketed and distant Mosquito Range, framed in the foreground with block-shaped Longs Peak, weathering the wind like a ship at sea. To the east, clear to Kansas, stretched the Great Plains in crystal air. To the west and north, we saw more rugged and storm-smothered ranges of western Colorado and southern Wyoming. But the air here remained momentarily clear and pure. It seemed that even a myopic person could dispense with his or her glasses.

Soon, however, advancing storm clouds swept in like a coastal fog, blurring our vision. Descending ever so carefully, our calf muscles began to ache, but icy boulders forced us to stay on mental alert every second of the way. When we reached the upper limits of tree line, big flakes of snow sprinkled down like confetti. The chirping of chickadees in the spruce woods blended with the roar of Fall River far below. Already it was getting warmer—the banana belt, we thought. When we reached the lodgepole forests, off came our sweaters. We arrived by late afternoon in the dying rays of sun at the cabin and were greeted by those who had prepared a Thanksgiving supper. A roaring log fire comforted us as we sat down to the tastiest turkey dinner of our lives, made all the more memorable with sage- and pine-nut-flavored stuffing.

PART II — MUMMIES IN SUMMER

On a bright August morning during my third season as a ranger, several of us took a day off to climb into the peaks of the 13,000-foot Mummy Range of Rocky Mountain National Park. From 8,000-foot Horseshoe Park one can clearly see the mummylike configuration of this mountain range by tilting one's head sideways. Six of the nine peaks all stood in view, with Hagues Peak (13,560 feet), the highest, dominating. Naturally, we selected Hagues as our challenge for the day. From its summit one is afforded a fine view of Rowe Glacier, the only glacier in the park above 13,000 feet.

We began our slow trek up the Lawn Lake Trail with our backpacks and canteens rattling in unison. In a matter of minutes, we gained altitude as the trail switched back and forth, giving us a broad view of flat-topped Deer Mountain. We rambled through peaceful groves of lodgepole pine and aspen, following the Roaring Fork River, which tumbled down from 11,000-foot Lawn Lake. Here a dam had been built before the national park was established to serve the purpose of water diversion for dryland farming in the prairies below. Some twenty years after our climb of Hagues Peak, this dam burst after a week of steady torrential rains in 1982. A wall of water roared down the canyon with boxcar-sized boulders that tumbled into Endo Valley, sounding like the end of the world. I would read about this in the *Mainichi Daily News* in Japan shortly before our climb of Mount Fuji. Canada jays screeched along the trail toward the base of jagged and glacially scarred Mummy Mountain (13,412 feet). Lower forests now gave way to dense, aromatic stands of Englemann spruce and silvery, sappy, subalpine fir. From here, amid scrubby spruce trees growing as mere bushes with bare roots clutching the soil, we gained a superb view of jagged Mummy Mountain rising above the bright and glaring waters of Lawn Lake. Heavily glaciated cliffs rose straight up to the sheer heights of Mummy and Fairchild (13,502 feet) mountains. In contrast, soft and delicate yellow marsh marigolds glistened in the wetlands nestled beneath cliffs resembling French Impressionist art.

    A shoreline ranger patrol cabin awaited us with a fireplace, some bunks, and a dirt floor. An icy spring gushed from the rocks just outside the cabin. We rested our weary bones after drinking some of that ice-cold spring water. Trout rose in the middle of the lake, tempting us to linger here all day long. But we methodically pushed on toward higher ground, following a steep trail out of Lawn Lake, and in no time we had trekked above tree line. A half hour later we stood and stared at Crystal Lake some 500 feet directly below us at the foot of Mount Fairchild. We took the saddle approach to Hagues Peak at 12,400 feet and thence up the cliffs for the next 1,100 feet. The snow-blanketed Never Summer Range constantly caught our eyes. But stubborn Hagues Peak still rose above.

    I came down with a sharp headache but continued to climb right up to the base of the peak until I began to feel a bit dizzy. In deference to me, we stopped for a rest on a flat boulder field some 13,200 feet high and ate our lunch. Tart-tasting lemonade and beef and pickle sandwiches proved to be just the right thing. I had no difficulty whatsoever springing up the final bit of cliff to the summit. From atop Hagues Peak, the pure white and wrinkled surface of Rowe Glacier hypnotized us. It nearly covered a modest-sized lake where the Big Thompson River begins. Rowe Glacier (formerly Hallett Glacier) was discovered by the Hallett Expedition in 1876, when it was twice as large as it is now. But it is still large, being about a quarter mile long and 100 feet high. Pale green pan ice continually forms on the lake during the summer months. Because this ice body is slowly moving over its own pressurized and plasticized interior, it is called a glacier; otherwise it would be merely a snowfield.

Staring at Rowe Glacier, I remembered well spending a day on the rugged surface of Paradise Glacier hugging the flanks of Mount Rainier, where I followed the banks of a clear, cold stream until it completely disappeared under the ice. There I rested a wee while enjoying a glacial symphony. Rivulets trickled, gurgled, and dripped like the abstract expressionistic music of Arnold Schoenberg. My mother, sitting on an ox-horn stool at my father's Parnassus Bookshop in Princeton, always used to say she hated Schoenberg's music. But had she heard these glacial drippings, who knows? Schoenberg himself was Austrian. Had he been inspired by irregular glacial drippings? Rocks constantly tumbled off the lava ridges of Rainier, sometimes rolling to within a few yards of where I stood daydreaming. I hiked a bit farther across the snowfield until I spotted an open patch of river down in the ice. Gingerly, I crawled deep into the hole some ten feet below within the white roof of a giant's mouth. Hunching over, I took a couple hundred steps into a bluish-white ice cave until I could no longer see the sky. Sitting down on an exposed rock fifteen feet under the base of Paradise Glacier, all sorts of thoughts whirled through my head. Even though I was as removed from humanity as I possibly could be, in here I felt a very strong sense of community. It was as though the stones in the stream were given eyes, and the icy water itself was given ears, and the lumpy inner layers of ice—a heart. My humanity became its voice, and its mountaineity became my mode of expression. If only for a few moments in the ice cave, I began to "think like a mountain," to use Aldo Leopold's words. When I emerged, Mount Rainier looked brighter than ever.

We gazed to the north beyond Rowe Glacier to see the Rawah Range and the upland prairies of southern Wyoming. On the horizon, through our binoculars, we could actually discern tiny dots of buildings in Laramie, Wyoming, some sixty air miles distant. Little did I realize that I would be living in one of those tiny dots for some twenty-five years, teaching at the University of Wyoming.

Since it was still only early afternoon, we decided to return via the summit of Mummy Mountain. The descent of the cliff proved to be relatively easy until we reached the top of a mile-long boulder field. Each and every boulder we stepped on wriggled and rocked, and after about thirty minutes of continually catching our balance, we sat down exhausted between Hagues and Mummy. Far underneath this boulder field, as well as underneath the one on Longs Peak, there has been discovered a vast network of black, quasi-underground glaciers that move gradually, causing this wobbly, rocky instability. As I stood up, I spotted a dead Clark's nutcracker, a large, jay-sized bird with gray, black, and white coloration. It was most surprising to see a dead one in that they are supposedly very strong fliers and rarely crash land. I imagine, though, the wind currents at this altitude can be quite treacherous.

Tired as I was, I felt every inch of the ground as we slowly ascended the rising slopes of Mummy Mountain. Fortunately, we walked along the gentle eastern slope of the mountain. Mummy Mountain, like most of the Colorado Rockies, has one side gashed out by the glaciers of the Wisconsin Ice Age some 10,000 years ago. It is this gashed-out side that is exposed to Lawn Lake. The other side is a gently rolling peneplain. Before long, we stood at the cairn marking the summit. Longs Peak rose across the way with its surrounding court, including Chief's Head and McHenry's.

Soon we bounced down the terraced slopes of the south flank and gradually descended into the stunted trees of timberline. Not being on a trail, we had a bit of difficulty keeping our bearings once we entered a dense forest. The Lawn Lake Trail had to be directly below us, but how far below we did not know. Naturally, when one *thinks* he or she is close to home at the end of a journey, he or she really is not, and such was our case. In order to get to our trail, we had to ford three streams, climb down two steep cliffs, and crawl through a briar patch. All this reminded me of my frantic state when

I was lost on Mount Ida a few years earlier. I had descended, during a violent thunderstorm, to a strange lake where no friends awaited me. I had to trample through trailless forests downhill to the Colorado River Valley for some eighteen hours before reentering civilization. But now, thankfully, we reached the Lawn Lake Trail. Our legs felt like pounded steel and our stomachs growled like wolves. With each thud of our mechanical feet on the homebound trail, we felt more and more like stiff Egyptian mummies. Perhaps the man who named these mountains was not thinking of their configuration alone.

CHAPTER THREE

ASIAN AND ALASKAN INTERLUDES

PART I   FUJI SAN: CLIMBING AMONG THE STARS

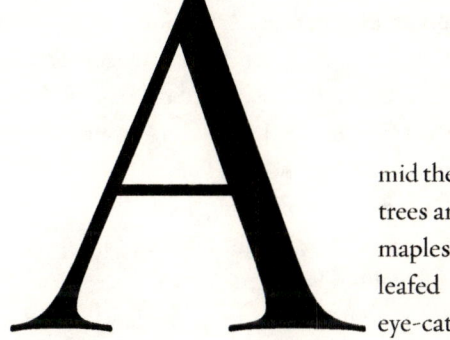

Amid the golden ginko trees and rich scarlet maples of autumn, I leafed through the eye-catching pamphlets describing the mystical mountain to the north. During the winter months, family, friends, and I had rambled over the hiking trails of a small extinct volcano called Kabutoyama (Helmet Mountain) and the nearby Rokko Mountains, which rise between Kobe and Osaka, where we lived for one brief year. Although the Rokko Mountains are indeed alluring, with their lush cedar forests, ferns, and occasional Buddhist temples, I still felt that to experience Japan completely, one must ascend Fuji San (Mount Fuji) to greet the rising sun.

Some of my colleagues argued that Fuji San (literally Origin Mountain) was nothing more than a tourist attraction. They felt that climbers had littered the trails so much that the mountain had become a mere sham of what it once was. Nonetheless, my desire to climb the mountain, sham or not, persisted. I immersed myself in Japanese art and culture and in the work of the famous woodblock-print artist Ichiryusai (or Ando) Hokusai, especially his tantalizing "Thirty-Six Views of Mount Fuji." One of my favorite of Hokusai's portrayals was the eighteenth view from Noboto Bay, in which the great, cone-shaped mountain of snow is seen from under a Buddhist *torii* (a gateway to a shrine). Fuji was gradually becoming for me a kind of shrine in itself, of a sort I did not fully comprehend.

During the height of the cherry-blossom season in early April, my family and I left for South Korea to meet an old friend and his family. I had not seen Jonny Boucher in twenty-four years, since back in Acadia National Park in Maine. We had climbed Mount Katahdin—of Thoreau fame—together then, and had planned a reunion this year in the form of climbing Mount Halla on Cheju-do Island, off the Korean Peninsula. Our climb of 6,398-foot Halla San, with its richly varied skirting forests, was magnificent, and our view out into the East China Sea contained colors and shapes worthy of a woodblock by Hokusai, but I still thought of this ascent merely as preparation for 12,388-foot Mount Fuji.

During the remainder of spring, back in flower-flooded Japan, we gradually planned our climb with our Japanese friend Yuko Kobayashi, who had not been on Fuji San since her early childhood. The overbearing, humid heat of early July, combined with the buzzing locusts and with my having to correct hundreds of final examinations of Osaka University students, made me wonder if Fuji were nothing more than a hazy illusion. How would I have the energy to climb such a mountain in all this heat?

Our date of departure brought dark clouds and light rain. Six of us walked down a steep hill to Nigawa's railway station to travel to Osaka Station, in order to board the *Shinkansen* (Bullet Train). I had never experienced such sweltering heat, and our heavy backpacks hardly helped. However, we all cooled off on the *Shinkansen* as we whirled through the Japanese countryside at 140 miles per hour. Tea plantations, rice paddies, and tile-roofed villages blurred past us, as if all were a dream.

At Shizuoaka we changed trains for Fujinomiya. A misty but not rainy Fuji rose miles above us and the surrounding rice fields. At Fujinomiya we boarded a *gogome* (fifth-station) bus and began to wind our way past lush green tea plantations and to gain altitude through pine and spruce forests. Eventually we arrived at the fifth station, at 7,200 feet—the same altitude as our home in Laramie, Wyoming. We changed our clothes, procured some walking sticks, and began our climb. Our nighttime destination was the eighth station (*hachigome*), at an altitude of 10,000 feet, where we would have dinner, stay overnight, and get up early the next morning to continue our ascent.

My wife Maura and I, our children, and Yuko hiked up the *unlittered*, steep, and winding trail past phantomlike strands of pine twisted by the elements. The mist thickened, and brief spits of rain hit our bodies and the volcanic dust at irregular intervals. The valleys below offered nothing but an endless sea of gray. Occasionally we had glimpses of a dark massiveness rising high above the trailing strands of upslope mist. Our backpacks began to seem heavy, and I started to feel like one of the old parents of Japanese legend who raised a young girl whose home was the moon. When she became twenty years of age, her aged foster parents climbed to the summit of Fuji San to return her to the moon. It felt as though *we* were climbing to the moon after a short rest at the sixth station (*rokugome*).

The mist thickened. I had the sensation that I had become part of the background in a Chinese scroll landscape painting by Ta Ch'ih or a contemporary. It began to rain harder, forcing us to cover our heads with plastic rain gear. My three children—Rich, Michelle, and Maureen—were tiring quickly, as was our Japanese friend, whose pack was immense. The ground became slippery, and loose volcanic chunks tricked our feet with every step. The seventh station (*sichigome*) was welcomed, but as it was becoming darker and rainier, we all wished that the seventh was the eighth!

We wearily checked into the eighth station at last, unloading our damp gear and walking in our stocking feet across wooden floors to an open charcoal pit, or *kotatsu*, to warm our hands. Yuko ordered six steaming bowls of *udon* (Japanese noodle soup) with mountain vegetables and rice. We kneeled at a low table and voraciously ate our alpine supper. Our breath added steam to the thick air of this stark room. The rain pounded down on the roof, and thankfully we were not still hiking the trail! The only warm place was either the charcoal pit or in one's sleeping bag, so we decided to turn in early, as we would be up at 3 a.m. to continue the climb. Apparently, 120 people had planned to sleep at the eighth station that night, but virtually all had cancelled due to the heavy rains. Our group of six, plus three older couples, were the only ones present on the chilly night of July 21, 1982.

I woke up freezing at 2 a.m. An old man snored heavily, and the echoes of his roaring filled the entire mountain barracks. I couldn't drift back to sleep and instead got up and walked out into a dazzling, starry night completely devoid of rain clouds. The stars gleamed overhead, and the small towns of Mishima and Fujinomiya near the eastern coast glowed far below like underworld constellations. Fuji looked as though it had become part of the Milky Way, with its upper snowfields blending into the heavens. I felt like Shimamura, a character in Yasunari Kawabata's famous novel *Snow Country*, as he stood outside in the hilly, wintry north country of Japan in silence:

> The Milky Way. Shimamura too looked up, and he felt himself floating into the Milky Way. Its radiance was so near that it seemed to him to take him up to it. Was this the bright vastness the poet Basho saw when he wrote of the Milky Way arched over a stormy sea?

I stood and stared until my teeth chattered. The promised warmth of the building finally pulled me back inside. By now the noisy old man was up, but my family and friend were still in a deep sleep. Crawling back into my sleeping bag, I quickly dozed off for a half hour or so until I heard a loud crunching sound. Maura awakened startled, and wondered if Fuji was becoming an active volcano again. Both of us dressed quickly and went outside to find hundreds of Japanese hikers with torchlights on their caps crunching up the mountainside from the fifth station, looking like mythical beings attempting to return to some sort of Japanese Shangri-La.

Astonished, Maura and I went back inside and discovered the rest of our group up and eating a breakfast of oranges, seaweed crackers, and hot green tea (*o'cha*). The first glow of morning light was already visible from far out in the Pacific as we hit the trail. Japan's rising sun is Colorado's setting sun. We slowly hoofed along toward luminous snowfields 2,000 feet above us. All of the valleys below had clouded in.

About 800 vertical feet above the eighth station, a Buddhist *torii* framed the rising sun. The *torii* glowed red and then gold above the black lava rocks. And then one of the most mystical alpine views of my experience suddenly sprung before me. The pyramid shape of Fuji San cast itself on the lower clouds and moved slowly westward. Only one time before had I seen this Brocken Specter (as John Muir called it in *The Mountains of California*), and that was on Longs Peak, Colorado, twenty-two years earlier.

Except for Maura, all of my climbing party were weary, tired, and sick. Realizing they were suffering from altitude sickness, I suggested we stop at the ninth station (*kugome*) for some restorative tea. It was warm and cozy there, with some lively but plaintive Japanese folksongs as background music.

Maura volunteered to stay at the ninth station (11,000 feet) with the sick ones while my restored daughter Maureen and I hiked up to the ninth and a half station and slowly and carefully picked our way along the lava trail to the tenth and final station. It was chilly at the summit of 12,388 feet but very exhilarating to peer down into the 600-foot-deep crater. The temperature at 8 a.m. was a blustering 34 degrees F. We ducked into a Buddhist *jinja*, or shrine, to warm up, and chatted in broken Japanese with one of the monks kneeling on the *tatami* mats of the highest shrine in Japan at *kugome* (tenth station). All of Honshu Island remained enshrouded in silver banks of cloud far, far below. But here, in the lodge of the sun, we stood humbly in the radiant brightness of crisp sky and white snow.

Maureen and I quickly bounced down the trail to the ninth station. Maura, Rich, Michelle, and Yuko were all feeling a bit better after imbibing cups of hot green tea. As we collectively dropped down to the eighth station, everyone's spirit improved. We rallied and chose to take a different route down the mountain, passing through lush red lava formations by means of narrow, convoluted chimneys that required a little rock work. All of lower Japan still lay salted away in mist and cloud. As we eased our way through the odd lava shapes of this bright-red section of Fuji, it reminded me of Hokusai's thirty-second view, "Summer Showers Beneath the Peak."

We finally had cleared the cliffs and, having let up our guard, trotted down a loose lava-gravel trail, when I suddenly slipped. The rubble rolled under me and I slid on my arm for about six feet. A nasty scratch scored my exposed skin, and my blood began dripping on rouge lava. The two women in our party came rapidly to my aid and poured water on my wound and applied bandages. At that moment, both my body and spirit became fused with this powerful mountain — it became an origin of myth for me for all my living days. Somehow I didn't mind at all making Fuji a tad bit redder.

Part II — The Snows of Halla San

We sailed out of a stormy Pusan Harbor early in the evening of April 3, 1982. The storm intensified as we passed the last flashing lighthouse and entered the Straits of Korea. My British friend, Jonny Boucher, and I paced the rain-pelted deck and watched the ship churn its way through rough, dark waters. Our vessel began to roll and pitch after one hour's sail, but this did not prevent us from checking a detailed map of Cheju Island. It was dominated by Halla San, the highest mountain in the Republic of Korea. We discussed our possible routes up the mountain to its 6,397-foot summit and reminisced over our last climb in 1958 of Mount Katahdin in the state of Maine when we had last seen each other.

Halla San is an extinct volcano that hasn't erupted for nearly a thousand years, and we hoped it would not become a sister to Mount Saint Helens during our brief visit. My friend and I and our wives chatted over a drink while trying to hold on to our chairs in our swaying cabin. Twelve hours later, after churning out of the Straits of Korea and into the East China Sea, we could make out the dim outline of Cheju Island in the early hours of dawn.

Approaching Cheju City Harbor, we failed to discern the slopes of Halla San, which were obscured in veils of cloud and mist. We chose to relax and see bits of the island the rest of this day and hoped for a sunny, clear day on April 5. It was pleasant to visit the small fishing village of Sagwipo, with its orange groves and South Sea Island–like waterfalls of Chonje-yon. But our real interest lay in climbing Halla San the next morning.

April 5 dawned clear. Halla San, crater and all, rose high into the sky. It looked like there was a dusting of snow on its upper slopes, but we couldn't be sure. We drove our car toward the trailhead on the east slope far above the Buddhist temple of Gwaneum-Sa with its hundreds of Buddhas seated in a semicircular amphitheater. We whisked past open fields of dry *susuki* grass and entered groves of cedar, where we parked our car. High above us rose the distant crater under clear skies. We started a very quick pace up through scrub oak, ash, and hemlock trees. Black rooks circled above the treetops as though we were back in Great Britain. A cock ring-necked pheasant strutted through the bush ahead of us—something I hadn't seen since being back in Wyoming and Nebraska.

The trail became quite steep and stony, and we soon lost our breath. We took a rest at the "virtuous tree," where the maiden of an ancient Korean king during a period of famine prayed at the base of the tree to have acorns come tumbling down as a kind of manna from above. Upward we climbed along spiny ridges that afforded us vast views of lower volcanic domes and the sparkling East China Sea. The grasslands below put me to mind of the eastern plains of New Mexico. The more I thought about it, the more it seemed to me that Cheju was a collection of little pieces of different parts of the world.

As we approached tree line and open alpine country, our attention was drawn to scrubby bushes laden with an intricate network of silvery ice crystals that seemed like a wintry scene in *Doctor Zhivago*. Above the ice crystals rose the silvered volcanic cone of Halla San, from which came blasts of chilly winds. We hiked across the windswept, grassy upper slopes to a hostel house to buy some fruit juice. This gave us a burst of much-needed energy, as the long, steep trail up to this point had tired us, and we had become quite thirsty. We chatted briefly with a Korean professor of English literature who had taken his students with him up this mountain in order to better appreciate Percy Bysshe Shelley's poem "Ode to Mont Blanc."

Jonny Boucher and I continued our trek by dipping down into a pine-studded ravine filled with frozen packed snow that was as hard as ice. Gingerly, we proceeded over the ice and up a rocky shoulder to the base of the frozen crater itself. We were ready for our final ascent. The upper mountain was ice-laden and steeped in mist. Looking up at the higher, dark pinnacles fringed with pines that were drooping with icicles, I thought we had become part of an oriental scroll painting.

The way up was steep and slippery. Frozen cables (as on Longs Peak) served as handholds in particularly difficult spots. When we were in the pineapple fields below, we hadn't realized how cold it would be up here, and we had failed to bring along gloves. Two Korean girls, coming down off the cone, noticed our red hands and very kindly offered their gloves to us. We said, *"kamsa hamnida"* numerous times to them and proceeded slowly and carefully up the icy steps that were carved in the rock underneath. Several times I gripped the cable tightly when I lost footing, but after much effort and carefully chosen steps, we arrived safely at the crater's summit to peer out into mist and fog 6,397 feet above the level of the sea. Although our bodies were weary, our minds and spirits had been invigorated by this unique Asian wilderness above the clouds on Cheju Island. Truly, as Henry David Thoreau contends, "In wildness is the preservation of the world."

PART III — A MISTY VIEW FROM MOUNT ROBERTS, ALASKA

> Piping sparrow and
> Raven call through mist hugging
> White Alaskan peaks

Samuel Young writes of his and John Muir's 1879 voyage along coastal Alaskan waters, "We camped at the site of what is now

Juneau, the capital of Alaska, and no dream of the millions of tons of gold that were to be taken from those mountains disturbed us." I sought a different gold as well 107 years later.

It wasn't difficult finding the trailhead above the city where soft rain angled down from the grayness of cloud. I cautiously proceeded along the Mount Roberts Trail through foggy forests of Sitka spruce, hemlock, yellow cedar, and alder. There were also thick undergrowths of stinging devil's club, ferns, mosses, and clusters of blue lupine and red Indian paintbrush. But quickly the trail became extremely steep with a series of tiring switchbacks. I rested for a spell and glanced down on Juneau Harbor, filled with fishing craft, luxury liners, and seaplanes taking off like buzzing mosquitoes through layers of fog. However, nature's own sounds held sway. Aisles of spruce resounded again and again with the musical quiver of rising notes from a Swainson's thrush, and splashing threads of waterfalls tumbled down the flanks of Mount Juneau, which was spun all over with webs of mist.

I plodded ever upward. From beneath my dripping poncho, I noticed how scrawny the trees had become; ferns had barely unfurled from damp fiddleheads. Notes from some distant thrush or warbler suddenly caught my ear, but the more I listened, the more I imagined them to be faint notes from a stone flute. One cannot help but feel the presence of the spirits of the Tlingit and Haida Indians in such a place as this. How fortunate Muir and Young were to have shared a portion of their lives with natives of Alaska a hundred years ago.

Mist cleared long enough for me to spot the glazed summits of Mount Gastineau and Mount Roberts looming above like humpback whales—only to disappear in grayness. An omnipresent wind shifted direction and blew gently across the valley, carrying the plash of many distant waterfalls. Was I in Scandinavia? The symphonic strands of Jean Sibelius' "Finlandia" kept racing through my mind.

Ever upward I hiked, through endless groves of leafy scrub alder bushes as if I were in a dream. Suddenly I was scared witless by a willow ptarmigan, fluttering and clucking like some mythological being, trying to decoy me away from her brood of chicks. With a fast-beating heart, I continued my climb onward across glaring snowfields that had been melted down to the green tundra of June. Here in panhandle Alaska, tree line is more than 10,000 feet lower than it is in Colorado—1,500 feet! A denizen of the tundra, the Smith's longspur, whistled a high note and then, a bit later, a low note. In the spirit of fun, I whistled two highs and a low, and various combinations of highs and lows, trying to confuse him. But, of course, he maintained his beauteous composition, claiming his territory.

Finding an exposed rock, I sat down to peer through holes in the fog at brilliantly illuminated peaks above the Juneau Ice Field. Time vanished up here in the Alaskan tundra; who knows how long I sat just staring at fog patterns that occasionally revealed alpine peneplains. Noticing how dark the tundra had become, I became apprehensive. Mountains no longer peeked through fog holes. Even the Smith's longspur ceased its song. Primal instinct warned me of an impending storm; quickly I descended to open tundra and alder clumps.

Sure enough, by the time I reached the scrub timber, it started to pour down in buckets, making my steep and muddy trail as slick as grease. I had to catch myself a couple of times; my feet nearly slipped from under me. Thankfully, I entered the firmer ground of a Sitka forest not so far above the silvery-wet streets of Juneau. As I looked out over the shining rooftops of that city, punctuated with the onion-top dome of a Russian Orthodox church, I did not wonder that John Muir returned for six more visits after 1879 to this land of misty ice and greenness.

CHAPTER FOUR

WHERE LAND IS MOSTLY SKY

PART I — GRAYS AND TORREYS LOOMING ABOVE

How clear it was that morning when three of us unloaded our gear from the car to climb two 14,000-foot peaks in central Colorado near Loveland Pass. It had been reported that the summit of Grays Peak experienced a short but furious burst of popcorn snow the day before. We all felt a little apprehensive about climbing two peaks on the same day. I hadn't climbed a fourteener since my thirty-fifth birthday almost twenty years earlier when I climbed Longs Peak for the third time. Now I was living in Denver, as were my two companions. Although we were all in our fifties, we remained, nonetheless, eager to climb two peaks in the high tundra where land is mostly sky. The jagged glacial ridge leading up to Grays and Torreys peaks jumped out at us in the clear air. It had an extraterrestrial look—all rock with just the slightest suggestion of green vegetation gleaming in the rising sun.

Down along our trail grew dense groves of willows, whose yellowing leaves gently rustled in the morning breeze. Ravens circled high above, following the contour of the surrounding glacial cirques. Father George Schroeder led and Mark Reames and I followed, sometimes stopping to admire Colorado columbines and sometimes craning my head back to look at billowing clouds that were taking on the shapes of the mountains underneath. George disappeared around the bend. By the time we reached him, he was on his knees in the subalpine grasses, not praying, but photographing a whole field of sun-glinted flowers that included yellow and rosy paintbrushes, bright-blue harebells, purple penstemon, and white bistort. "Vincent Van Gogh would have gone wild here," I remarked, and George answered with a grin.

By now, subalpine willows grew as mere mats huddled down low as much as possible out of the constant wind. We noticed some white dots above. Were they mountain goats or just rocks? At last they moved. We continued trekking along the trail and stopped frequently to catch our breath, as we were now well above 12,000 feet. People above us stood still, looking intently at something. Huffing and puffing, we arrived at their level on the mountain to see a female mountain goat in a shaggy coat with her three kid goats all staring directly at us. Jagged peaks had come into view to the north and east along with several other fourteeners, including Mount Bierstadt and Mount Evans to the east of us and Longs Peak to the far north. We could also make out several high thirteeners like Arapaho Peak and Square Top. One year earlier, Mark Reames and I had sauntered up 13,400 foot Arapaho Peak, with its jagged summit looming over the wrinkled mass of Arapaho Glacier, the water source for the city of Boulder. Mark recalled that this glacier had receded considerably since the early 1940s. Soon we could not see anything to the south and west save the high, looming slopes of Grays directly above and Torreys to our right. We had to climb still higher to cast an eye on the Collegiate Range with Mounts Princeton, Harvard, and Yale.

The soil under our feet appeared sparse and stony. A few tufts of alpine forget-me-nots coated the immediate foreground. From such a perch it was easy to agree with John Muir that the mountaineer climbed mountains with more than his or her feet and hands:

> In like manner the soul sets forth at times upon rambles of its own. Our bodies, though meanwhile out of sight and forgotten, blend into the rest of nature, blind to the boundaries of individuals. But it is after both body and soul of a mountaineer have worked hard, engaged hard, that they are most palpably separate. Our weary limbs, lying at rest on the pine needles, make no attempt to follow after or sympathize with the nimble spirit, that apparently glad of the opportunity, wanders along down gorges, along beetling cliffs, or away among the peaks and glaciers of the farthest landscapes, or into realms the eye had not seen, nor ear heard; when at length we are ready to return home to our flesh-bone tabernacle, we scarcely for a moment or two know in what direction to seek for it.

But *our* bodies reminded us that they were thirsty and hungry. The summit looked insurmountable. It seemed to rise higher and higher. We now stood above 13,000 feet, and it had become chilly, but not so chilly as to make us put on jackets. In the bracing air, we slowly edged a bit higher to walk out onto a promontory ridge where we caught whiffs of fresh forest air from lower depths. Longs Peak looked close enough to hit it with a stone.

More mountain goats gathered on rocky ledges below us. Their beards fluttered in the steady breezes. Alpine flowers, looking like miniature fiery suns, bobbed on their stalks, and tailless pikas squeaked in high pitch, punctuating our alpine flow of thoughts. I could discern tiny human figures apparently standing on the top of Grays Peak, recalling my ascent of Mount Fuji in which droves of Japanese pilgrims hung over the edge of the volcanic peak to shout words of encouragement to climbers lower down. Mark Reames, who had lived in Japan for more than twenty years, read my thoughts, saying, "No teahouse here to refresh us!" Seeing a marmot scurry along the trail encouraged us to keep pace, slow though it was.

We arrived at the point where there was nothing but sky all around the rocky ridge just ahead. That ridge eventually yielded until we stood on top in a little circle of rocks surrounded by a universe of endless mountain ranges.

The Mount of the Holy Cross rose to the far southwest, as well as scores of other peaks of the Sawatch Range, including distant Shavano and Antero. And to the extreme southwest, we just barely discerned the hazy Maroon Bells and heavily glaciated Snowmass Peak. Like Buddhist monks high in the Himalayas, we turned slowly in circles, absorbing the cosmos, until a sudden shower of popcorn snow caught us by surprise and coated our hair as white as mountain goats. We smiled. All this reminded Mark of his experiences in the Japanese Alps, which were inhabited by white snow monkeys. He loved to watch them scramble across bright snowfields.

Out came our sandwiches and juice. We ate heartily amid an August snowstorm at 14,270 feet atop Colorado's ninth highest peak. During our lunch, several shaggy mountain goats outstared us with their shiny, dark eyes. Far below we could see a little piece of Interstate 70, with its mad scramble of ant-sized cars heading for the Eisenhower Tunnel. Although we could not see the entrance to the tunnel, we could readily observe the buzzing ants' destination—the wide valley containing Lake Dillon and several ski areas and a very dark puff of cloud that would probably surprise the ants once they got through the tunnel.

George, Mark, and I were game to go ahead with our plan to ascend a second fourteener that loomed a half mile west of us. We would have to descend a thousand feet or more to the saddle and then painfully regain the elevation lost. Torreys Peak is only three feet lower than Grays. Of course, the scramble down to the saddle was a cinch, except for a few wobbly rocks. The sun broke through the clouds—a welcome sight as we passed by several crusty snowfields at the saddle and slightly above us. And then, as Torreys' pitch increased, I felt my muscles tire—no wonder, after climbing Grays Peak a short while ago. All I could see was rock and sky as we slowly edged toward the summit.

We paused to catch our breath by photographing a sparkling

snowfield or a bright cluster of yellow lichen that coated the boulders. Breathing became difficult. Perhaps the combination of Grays and Torreys was beginning to take its toll. I began to doubt my strength. Was I going to make it? Where were George and Mark? Had they vanished into thin air?

And then I realized that they stood on the summit just overhead. They weren't miles away after all. A few huffs and puffs and I saw their faces. A few more, and I saw their entire bodies against the sky. They stood among a herd of mountain goats, and George was talking to them: "Thank you, gentlemen, for sharing your marvelous home with us!"

After resting five minutes at 14,267 feet and drinking some cold water, we all felt restored and energetic. Several other climbers joined us and engaged us in a discussion about which mountain range was which and which ski area was Breckenridge as opposed to Keystone. Mark, the native Coloradan, settled these issues with a tone of finality. Before making our descent, we cast one more glance around the universe of alpine terrain that consisted of lower reddish ridges, distant gray peaks, azure-blue skies with cumulus clouds, and the distant mass of Mount Evans and Mount Bierstadt to the east, perhaps twenty-five miles away. We tentatively agreed to climb one more fourteener, probably Mount Bierstadt, after a two-week sojourn in the city of Denver somewhere far below. We waved goodbye to our fellow mountaineers (both humans and goats) and began our rapid descent to the saddle between the peaks.

Halfway down to the saddle, it began to snow, only more furiously than atop Grays Peak. The sky had become completely gray and the winds increased. Instead of going all the way down and around the base of Grays, we looked for cutoff trails down the hollow bowl between the peaks. I followed the crest of a snowfield while my two companions took a surer route along the bottom edge of the snow. I told them I would meet them down yonder where the snowfield trail and the talus trail joined, perhaps 800 vertical feet below.

Just a month earlier, I had climbed Saint Mary's Glacier above Idaho Springs to the green tundra. I had stopped and stared at a grazing cow elk some fifty yards distant. When it came time to descend the glacier with its steep pitch, I instinctively had traversed from one side to the other instead of going straight down and risking a slip. Today I felt quite comfortable on this snowfield, even though it had a rather steep drop-off to jagged rocks eighty feet lower. Apparently the dizzy angle had frightened away Mark and George.

As I traversed the steep snow patch and angled down toward naked rocks, I noticed that George and Mark had only begun their descent into the bowl. The increased wind and snowfall had me worried just a bit, especially when a conversation I had with my neighbor came to mind. She said she had slipped and slid upside down on one of these snowfields but fortunately had arrived headfirst harmlessly on grassy tundra. I kept moving with caution until all three of us edged closer to the rendezvous point in a mixture of driving sleet and snow. The going was nasty, and I was glad to be down in the glacial bowl, out of the wind. We were all close enough to talk to each other with our voices echoing off talus. "How's your trail?" I shouted. "Slick as grease," they shouted back. Before long, we no longer needed to shout. My trail descended rapidly over muddy rills and wobbly rocks. Quite a barren place, I thought to myself, as I hadn't noticed so much as one flower.

It was good to rejoin my companions. Grays and Torreys looked like monstrous giants about to hurl lightning bolts at us. Eventually, though, we walked through more grass than rock, and happily our trail joined the main route off Grays Peak. The sun returned full strength, and we stopped to take off our icy, hooded parkas and gulp down some very refreshing water from our canteens. Since we had expended much energy, both psychic and physical, the relatively simple descent proved wearisome. George stopped suddenly. We caught up with him and knew why. We listened to the wind in the willows. The sound varied in intensity and pitch with each new gust of wind. Ravens sailed above, following the wind currents. Willows, wind, and birds soothed our minds and made us forget the pain of our tired feet. We became three-winged Mercuries descending the last slope with a message of the mountain's glad tidings.

Part II — A Symphony of Storms

Mount Bierstadt, rising just west of Mount Evans, was named after German-born artist Albert Bierstadt (1830–1902). One of the last artists of the Hudson River School of painting, his works are characterized by vast panoramas of the Rocky Mountain West. I remember standing in front of one of his Wagnerian scenes at the Buffalo Bill Center in Cody, Wyoming. A horrendous lightning storm arched itself between two gigantic peaks of the Wind River Mountains of Wyoming. I believed that I could actually hear the wind, taste the rain, and feel the crackle of electricity, even though I stood in a warm museum. Although the vegetation was wrong, and the mountains absurdly high, the mood and atmosphere were right. The painting brought me back to my own experiences in thunderstorms in the Snowy Range of southern Wyoming. Nowhere else does the thunder boom and echo louder.

Twelve days after our climb of Grays and Torreys, Father George Schroeder and I and two new climbing companions, Willy Sutton and Ike Rodman, met at the little town of Grant, Colorado, at 8 a.m. to drive up to Guanella Pass and climb Mount Bierstadt (14,036 feet). The mountain would live up to its namesake by providing us with a Wagnerian overture.

At Guanella Pass, we were not certain which trail would lead us to Bierstadt's summit. The reason? A half dozen trails meandered into thick groves of willows that dropped from the 11,600-foot pass to 11,000 feet or so in the vale between us and the base of the summit. We decided to bushwhack our way through, sometimes feeling like Humphrey Bogart aboard the *African Queen* in search of the main channel of the Bora River to Lake Victoria. Just when we thought we found a way, the willows thickened up. George, wearing alpine short pants, fell into a hollow and almost disappeared completely. By the time we got to him, he had already managed to pull himself up on his feet while laughing all the while. Realizing he was not hurt, we all joined in with laughter.

At the bottom of the vale some five or six hundred feet lower than the pass, we forded a stream, sunk ankle-deep in subalpine marshes, and backtracked several times around incredibly thick clumps of willows. All of this could have been avoided if we had simply gone over to the northern part of Guanella Pass and picked up the established trail, which even has wooden walkways across marshy areas. Nonetheless, we forged up the willowy base of Bierstadt until we arrived, at last, on relatively free and open tundra at perhaps 12,000 feet. Grays and Torreys had nothing like this. Their approaches seemed relatively simple in comparison. At least the snowfields had not scratched our legs and arms.

Willy and I stopped frequently to photograph flowers and catch our breath. Willy coined a name for the Russian thistles that covered the side of the mountain. He called them eclipse flowers because they looked like a bunch of miniature dark eclipses with the morning sun behind them. Between the spiny thistles grew bright-red Indian paintbrushes, and down in hollows of rock, a cluster of dwarf columbines helped create a tundra palette with colors enough for the western artist Jacob Alfred Miller or Albert Bierstadt himself. A circular pattern of crusty green lichens a foot and a half in diameter smothered the side of a rock and looked quite literally like an artist's palette. Such a growth could easily be 150 years old. It served as a "base camp" for future mosses that, in turn, would collect dusts and soils. Perhaps a few hundred years from now, tundra flowers and dwarf willows will sprout forth from this rock.

Willy tapped me on the shoulder and said to look around. I had been so involved with the tundra before me that I had failed to notice how high we had climbed. To the west, in dark shadows, rose the twin peaks of Grays and Torreys. On the day we climbed them, Torreys Peak looked far more rugged than Grays, but from this distant perspective, we could see the jagged, south-facing side of Grays, which clearly matched the rugged, north-facing slope of Torreys, the side we had been exposed to during our ascent twelve days ago.

To the southwest we could make out the peaks of the Sawatch Range, but our view to the east remained obscured by the ever-rising slope of Bierstadt. George and Ike rested on rocks a hundred yards or so beyond us. They looked like two alpine mammals of some sort, so much did they blend into space. Ike and George continually discussed the existence of God, Ike being the doubter. Father George could not have had better props to argue in God's favor than the sublimity of an immense alpine panorama surrounding and dwarfing us all.

After frequent stops to catch our breath and admire close up the "eclipse" thistles, with their heads bent downslope, and minute cushions of purple phlox, we caught up with Ike and George in the midst of their dialogue at the saddle between a false summit and looming Mount Bierstadt. Here we could finally see the massive, tundra-clad Mount Evans rising to the east and a deep, rocky gorge containing Abyss Lake. The gorge served as an echo chamber for the high-pitched squeaks of tiny, rabbitlike pikas that were scampering on lower ledges. We estimated that we stood at about 13,000 feet. Several years later, my wife Maura and I, along with our little cocker spaniel Mini, would ascend the West Arm of Mount Evans along frighteningly steep ledges across the way. And Mini and I would climb Bierstadt a year later on a cold and windy Labor Day. At the summit, we would huddle together for warmth behind a windbreak of rocks.

But on this summer day, Willy and I joined George and Ike to push ahead, with the false summit gradually sinking behind us. Thunder rattled. Rock slabs rose above, and I knew then that we had arrived at a point where land is mostly sky. We waved a weary hello to other hikers and walked over to the summit's northern edge. We peered down several thousand feet into a rugged glacial cirque containing Abyss Lake. Thunder boomed all around us, and the skies had darkened dangerously. But the sun shone down on us. Father George said rather whimsically—for Ike's benefit—that if the Red Sea parted for Moses.... A mixture of rain and snow zoomed in on us while lightning bolts danced in the skies not too far away. We took some photographs and quickly dashed down the trail to a rocky shelter where we could eat our lunch.

Mount Bierstadt lived up to its name. As we sat huddled between 13,000 and 13,500 feet, torrents of rain with lightning etched the sky to the south, while an equally impressive storm zeroed in on the nearby mountains to the north. Bearing down on us from the west came a third storm. But where we sat, the sun beamed down on us as though we had been placed right inside a Bierstadt canvas.

We feasted on a communal lunch. Willy sliced his garden-fresh zucchini squash, which served as bread. I sliced my delicatessen feta cheese, George shaved off pieces of spicy salami, and Ike peeled his oranges. Willy served as the assembler of zucchini sandwiches. We ate faster than Willy's hands could move, but he continued to produce satisfying morsels until we had gorged ourselves. There was enough left over to feed several mountaineers. Father George paralleled our 13,000-foot feast with Christ's multiplication of loaves. The principle of sharing multiplied tenfold the joy of hungry men eating, which, in turn, dissipated fears of inevitable storms.

We got up on our stiff legs and picked up a clearly marked trail that dropped off at an almost dangerous pitch down to the valley of willows. We didn't want to get blasted by lightning and made a very fast descent. Within an hour, we were thrashing our way through willows dampened with rain. I looked up at Bierstadt, covered in mist and cloud. It looked higher than Mount Everest from this willow jungle. I couldn't imagine a better way to have intensified and energized our lives than these few hours above the din of our daily travail.

CHAPTER FIVE

4-CORNER HIGH

Part I — Uinta Unity

My companions prepared for the Uintas, each in his own way. Mark Reames practiced hiking with his new backpack days before our excursion into eastern Utah. Willy Sutton camped in southern Utah, photographing some little-known winding and narrow canyons, while I finished teaching a summer class in Rocky Mountain National Park. We all had the Uintas on our mind; there we would climb for twenty-five miles in the only major range of mountains in the Rocky Mountain West that runs east-west and not north-south—the Uinta Range.

The Uintah Utes believe that these mountains are sacred because their base is surrounded by a circle of red sandstone. They believe that when this world comes to a violent geologic end, survivors will assemble within the sacred ring of Uinta sandstone to form a new tribe of what was once Turtle Island, or North America.

The Uintas have a unity all their own. Perhaps they were, according to University of Wyoming geologist Professor Carol Frost, part of a much older plate (up to 3.9 billion years old) around which other plates gathered. This much older plate, made up of the bulk of present-day Wyoming, northern Utah, and eastern Nevada, could have been the original Turtle Island, bedecked with palms and tropical coves, billions of years before humans were around. Some tribal people of the Great Plains believe, according to A.C. Ross of Pine Ridge, South Dakota, that humans have been in North America for millions of years but as disembodied spirits. Those ancient spirits became familiar with each and every notch on the mountain ridges of the giant turtle's back.

Why do the Uinta Mountains run for 100 miles east to west, unlike all other major Rocky Mountains? A good question. It is curious that Split Mountain, Utah, to the east, is swirled, if not twisted, toward the Uintas. Several geologists have speculated about their east-west orientation. Philip B. King in *The Evolution of North America* (1959) believes that they are a Middle Proterozoic sedimentary formation that was originally part of the Siberian–North American rift zone, which was subsequently uplifted more than 13,000 feet. King wrote, "Like the Uinta Mountains themselves, the Uinta Mountain Group (including environs) extends eastward, and it probably accumulated in an aulocogen, or rift in the continental platform like the Precambrian–early Cambrian of the Wichita system in Oklahoma." A later-day geologist, John D. Cooper, in *A Trip Through Time* (1986), agreed with King that the Uintas are part of an aulocogen, or "failed rift," between Siberia and North America, which were east and west of each other. Today, however, Carol Frost has cast some doubt on the rift theory in that this old core plate is from 3.5 to 3.9 billion years old. Lands on both sides of the Pacific are younger, not older. The Rockies, for instance, are infants of only 60 million years. There is still the question of why the Uintas (having quartzite older than 2.5 billion years) run east to west, unlike the Wind Rivers of Wyoming, the Wasatch Mountains of Utah, the Sawatch Range of Colorado, and the Front Range of Colorado. Perhaps they are like Robert Frost's "West-Running Brook":

> What does it think it's doing running west
> When all the other brooks flow east
> To reach the ocean? It must be the brook
> Can trust itself to go by contraries.

The Uintas must trust themselves going by contraries, and therein lies their unity.

Mark and I had to meet Willy in Vernal, Utah, by 6 p.m. We, nonetheless, stopped for lunch two hours out of Denver on Vail Pass. There we sat in silence, watching strands of clouds gather like modern glaciers filling up the hanging valleys of the Front Range. Rosy paintbrushes and purple larkspur scented the fields before us. Distant Torreys Peak, which we had climbed the year before, darkened in a gray and threatening sky.

Mystical mist continued to collect on the rocky ledges of Glenwood Canyon and along the volcanic dikes north of Rifle as we journeyed on toward Vernal. We passed through a violent thunderstorm, with hail splatting against our windshield, near Dinosaur National Monument on the Colorado–Utah border, making for one of the wettest deserts I had ever seen or smelled. After a rain, gray sagebrush and juniper and pinyon pines scent the desert air like the most delightfully pungent of incenses in a Buddhist temple. Desert air revitalizes the soul. In the desert, the mind is led skyward, to a sky that is robbed of all moisture by the dry terrain below.

The twisting box canyons of a tan-brown Split Mountain allured us more than any siren of ancient times. We wanted to stop the car and get out to see what was what, but we had to meet Willy and make camp on the north slope of the Uintas, a hundred miles farther down the road.

With steak in our bellies, we three left Vernal for Manila, thence traveled westward to Henry's Fork via a small patch of southwestern Wyoming. On the way up into the mountains, while Willy filled us in on his experiences in southern Utah, we caught a glimpse of something. There in the lodgepole pines stood three or four circles of male Indians (Uintah Utes) holding hands in the dark of the night. Were they about to ghost dance? Was this the end of the world and the gathering of survivors? Their shiny black hair glistened in the moonlight. I felt a twinge of homesickness for the Wind River Indian Reservation and my old Shoshone friend Rupert Weeks, who once told me a story of his great uncles coming back from Fort Hall, Idaho, in the 1880s. On their return to Wyoming, they and others performed a ghost dance. When they all awakened the next day, they had somehow gotten five miles closer to home!

Closer to Henry's Fork, we drove slowly through an elk herd—perhaps one hundred elk pranced through the woods near the highway. Their eyes and white rumps gleamed in the lowering rays of the moon. Mule deer romped gracefully from tall grasses to cross our road; we had to go slow here in such a crowded city of wildlife. Mark spotted our turnoff for Henry's Fork, and we bounced over a dirt road into the forests of the Uintas of extreme northeastern Utah. It felt good to pull up to a campsite and even better to set up our tents and crawl into our sleeping bags in the frosty air.

The morning dawned clear but cold—ice cold. The tent had an outer layer of frost too thick to scratch off; the picnic table looked more white than brown. Was this Utah in mid-July? It sure as heck wasn't the Utah Willy had camped in a few days ago down by the Arizona line, with warm days and balmy evenings. We imagined that the Earth had decided to shift its axis. As we drank our coffee, holding the mugs closely for warmth, an ungainly female moose picked her way through the willows to within forty feet of us. Even she looked cold, with her puffs of breath steaming the air. She had a bluish tinge to her tan-gray coat.

Staring done, we packed forty pounds of gear and supplies into each of our frame packs and began a seven-mile hoof up to Dollar Lake to set up an alpine camp from which we would make our assault on Kings Peak, the highest in Utah. Within minutes we passed through bright fields of rosy paintbrushes and American bistort (whose root is edible), and on into tall stands of lodgepole pines, where we saw delicate clusters of white geraniums and yellow arnica (whose sepals give relief for rheumatism). Gurgling streams trickled through quiet groves of aspen, where we spotted the amazingly intricate work of beavers—neatly stacked aspen logs damming portions of feeder streams going into Henry's Fork. Enos Mills, father of Rocky Mountain National Park, wrote in *Wildlife on the Rockies* that a beaver dam was of great value in that "it spreads out or distributes the water of the few rainy days through all the days of the year. A river which flows steadily throughout the year is of inestimable value to mankind." Mills also noted, "So far as I know, the upper course of every river in the Rockies is through a number of beaver meadows, some of them acres in extent." The dams we passed by were works of art like a neatly interwoven carpet, providing a harbor for trout, deer, birds, and frogs—a city in the wild.

Our trail rose gently from 9,500 feet to a little over 11,000 feet over the course of seven miles. But gentle as it was, we had to give our bodies frequent rests. One time we stopped on a bluff overlooking Henry's Fork River, which flowed through lodgepole pines mixed with subalpine firs. Another time we rested on a footbridge. The icy river gushed beneath us, soothing our minds. We began to notice the wide glacial cirques of the Uintas with maroon-colored ridges to our left and right. The ridge closest to us and to our east rose steadily up to Gilbert Peak at 13,442 feet; to the west rose Flat Top Mountain at 12,170 feet. But we could not yet discern the head of the valley and Kings Peak. As western song sparrows and thrushes filled the air with melody, I kept thinking that we were about to enter an ancient harbor of some prehistoric world.

The Red Creek quartzite, for which the Uintas are famous, became more apparent the higher we climbed. According to Professor Carol Frost, some of this rock formation dates back to 2.5 billion years and more; that's more than five times older than the Appalachians. The concept of Turtle Island hit home. The Uintas are older, more mature pieces of the turtle's shell that has spread to Florida. Put mud on a turtle's back and the ridge lines do look like tectonic plates. Onward we forged through fir forests and across marshy meadows with globe flowers and marsh marigolds and, unfortunately, nagging mosquitoes.

Over one alpine rill, and there they rose! The high Uintas, all maroon colored with cathedral-organ-shaped cliffs looming skyward to white bands of snow and ice. We could readily discern the sedimentary layers of rock thrusted upward over millions of years into the pure air of 13,000 feet. In *Basin and Range*, John McPhee asked Professor Deffeyes of Princeton University about the strange configuration of the Uintas. According to Deffeyes:

> The north side of the Uintas is a spectacular mountain wall. Glorious. You come upon it and suddenly you see structurally the boundary of the range. But you don't see what put it there. The Uintas are mysterious. They are not a basin-range fault block, yet they have come up nearly vertically, with almost no compression evident. You stand there and watch them go up into the sky. They don't fit our idea of plate tectonics. The Rockies in general will be one of the last places in the world to be deciphered in terms of how many hits created them, and just when, and from where.

"The Uintas are mysterious" is the key. Wherever we looked, there were masses of layered red rocks, some of them looking like stepping stones to heaven. Once we had our tents set up in the woods above Dollar Lake, we ambled out into the valley to stand and stare. We could see the edge of Mount Gilbert and the flank of Flat Top Mountain and the challenging slopes of Kings Peak rising all the way up to 13, 528 feet above the current seas. Kings Peak, from our vantage point, looked like the jagged edge of a tin can sticking up after being opened with a pocket knife. A small troop of Boy Scouts from Salt Lake City and their leaders came trudging by.

"Have you ever climbed Kings?" I asked.

"Last year," the troop leader replied. "We didn't get back till midnight, and the only way we did that was to have the kids slide down snowfields into this valley. If we had followed the trail back, we'd *still* be on it a year later. It's a long ways back to that peak."

"Where ya settin' up for the night?"

"Henry's Fork Lake, up yonder."

"Gonna climb Kings again?"

"Gonna try."

We knew we were in for some hard work the next day, but at least we'd be carrying only day packs, not forty-pounders. The setting sun reddened the already ruffled red ridges around us, making a perfect Martian scene—Mars with a myriad of birds, that is.

By our mosquitoey fire that night we ate some stew and nibbled on trail mix, all the while chatting about Kings Peak. Would we have the energy? Two of us were well over fifty. What if it poured down rain? What if it snowed? How much grub should we take up there? Should we stick to the trail all the way or try snowfields coming back down? I guess I dreamed about these questions as I fell asleep above the silvery, moonlit waters of Dollar Lake fringed with evergreens thrumming in the evening breezes.

Not so cold the next morning, I thought to myself as I scrambled out of my sleeping bag. Robins chirped just like in my backyard in Denver. The sky? Crystal clear. And those mountains? Glorious. Mark, Willy, and I wolfed down bread and honey, cereal, and coffee and threw some oranges, bread, and candy bars into our packs. Onward and upward we paced toward Gunsight Pass at 11,800 feet. After Willy had taken several pictures, he volunteered some comments about the art of photography. He hoped to get some pieces of magic recorded on his film. Those pieces of magic in between countless other attempts are what give the photographer the impetus to keep shooting. It is a collection of those pieces of magic that the photographer gives to humankind to help in our understanding of what constitutes reality. Magical realism is not something out of Latin American fiction, where mythological realities fuse with daily reality. It could be a Mormon fritillary moth fertilizing an alpine blossom with his fuzzy antennae in the high Uintas—a kind of moth-person like a kachina spirit helping keep alive our green planet.

"What could it be?" I asked out loud.

"It could be almost anything," Willy responded. A magical moment makes a reality that has as much versimilitude as Henry James' notion of realism. Versimilitude has to take in meta-realities beyond drawing-room conversation. What is meta-reality? Geology, for one thing, and mythology for another. It is like the distant siren a canine hears or the faint grinding of tectonic plates a panda bear detects just before an earthquake, or the vision of survivors who will gather in the Uintas.

Gunsight Pass rose just ahead as we cleared the last scrubby stands of fragrant spruce and fir. At last we rambled over Utah tundra, our first ever in that state. Mark gleefully pointed down to some white alpine forget-me-nots; usually they were blue. Alpine sunflowers, the largest flower of the tundra, all pointed eastward toward the rising sun. Clusters of blue columbine hid among the dark crevices of trailside rocks. The air up there was exhilarating; each breathful was elixir to our lungs. No real clouds accumulated westward yet, and Gilbert Peak looked so clear that you could stretch your arm across Gunsight Pass and touch it. A few switchbacks and two snowfields later, we sat down at windy Gunsight Pass to eat a candy bar with no middle-aged qualms of guilt about how fattening chocolate is.

From up here we could see northward to the flat stretches of green plains and brown desert of my old home state of Wyoming. Somewhere out there, perhaps, a Basque shepherd was glancing up into the rugged Uintas and the cool white snowfields. Each vantage point offered meta-realities. To the south spread glacial valleys and winding ridges down into the heart of the Uintah Ute Reservation. Its boundaries now extend appropriately to where we sat. We could not see Kings Peak, as a cathedral-organ-shaped mountain blocked our view. Pipits winged past us, resisting the forceful gusts of wind and making for moments of magic on the film of our brains. If I had been a pipit, I don't know that I could have had any control in all that wind with my fluttering gray feathers. Time to move on.

We followed the spongy, wet trail to Anderson Pass and Kings Peak. But the trail descended! We did not want to go down, just to go up again. Nonetheless, we didn't wish to scramble across loose scree to a possible dead end high above and therefore dutifully followed the trail down to an alluring meadowland full of flowers and willows and trickling brooks. The soil was spongy and we hopped like toads through stygian lands dwarfed by the massive peaks of an upper world. The smell of fresh plants permeated our valley. Thoreau described the scents of a New England marsh in his *Journal*:

I perceive some of that peculiar fragrance from the marsh at the Hubbard Causeway, though the marsh is mostly covered. Is it a particular compound of odors? It is more remarkable and memorable than the scent of any particular plant,—the fragrance, as it were, of the earth itself.

We took a shortcut through the marsh by heading directly toward Anderson Pass, once we determined its location to the northwest. Kings Peak looked impossibly rocky and gigantic. I even suggested following a contour line up the back side of the mountain instead of going all the way to Anderson Pass, but upon closer examination, my suggested route appeared to be absolutely treacherous.

No clouds yet. Now began our uphill trek to Anderson Pass. It reminded me somewhat of the pathway up Medicine Bow Peak near Laramie, Wyoming, which my family and I had taken each Labor Day for twelve years straight. But Anderson Pass rests considerably above 12,000 feet, and the very top of Medicine Bow Peak is barely over 12,000 feet. We knew that once we stood on Anderson Pass, our troubles would begin. We would have a whole mountain to climb. My water supply was running a bit low, and I should never have taken a piece of sweet candy from Mark; it made me intolerably thirsty. I felt that I was losing energy fast, and Anderson Pass looked miles away. Thankfully, we all stopped for a much-needed rest by rivulets of icy snowmelt coming off Kings Peak.

Within several hundred feet, the tundra leveled off again, and thankfully, the going was easier. In fact, I led the way to the base of a large snowfield just below Anderson Pass. Here we ate lunch, although I was more thirsty than hungry. We looked down on the valley containing Dollar Lake and the headwaters of Henry's Fork River and could see the incredibly steep chute the Boy Scouts had slid down the year before. We felt the chill of the snowfield and proceeded onward, if only to warm up. Cautiously, we picked our steps through watermelon-smelling snow (thoroughly laced with a poisonous-to-humans red algae). Willy was the first to make it to the top of the pass.

"Hey, we're at 12,700 feet!" Willy shouted.

"Are you sure it isn't 12,200 feet?" I asked.

"Read the sign!"

Truly, we all stood at 12,700 feet, some 500 feet higher than I had expected. That information gave me a boost. We had only 828 vertical feet to go—a mere eighty-storey office building the likes of the Chrysler Building in New York.

Still no sign of clouds over that vast Utah sky. Willy got a kick out of my newfound energy and bounded ahead, picking his way along a barely visible trail, over loose rock slabs of shale shining in the sun and darker granite boulders. It's one thing to follow a winding trail over tundra and quite another to make rapid progress up rock cliffs, past dizzying overhangs, with nothing but sky all around.

High-pitched squeaks of pikas filled the air as Utah spread before us. We could begin to make out the distant, swirling canyons of Split Mountain back on the Colorado border. We glanced down at the High Line Trail, winding over pass and gorge, running the length of the Uintas. At one point it looked as narrow as a pathway along a steel girder high above Manhattan. The trail snaked along an almost vertical pitch on the back side of Red Castle Mountain. One miscalculation and you'd be history. Willy and I stopped to make sure Mark was coming along alright. When he waved, we proceeded up to a false summit, only to see the high, jagged block of Kings still a ways up there.

Although there were not as many flowers around us as there were on the tundra, the beauty and diversity of the rocks made up for it. We could see in any direction granites, shales, quartzites, and sandstones, all with a reddish-brown hue. Deep within the rocks we could hear the gurgle of underground springs and streams, and we wondered about the dark interior of these mountains. Was there a network of watery channels inside possible caverns? Willy tried to capture pieces of magic by stopping here and there to compose photographs ever so carefully, sometimes ever so precariously, near the western edge of Kings Peak high above the linear geosynclines of the Uintas.

It was fun working our way up to the true summit. There were ample grips on the rocks above. Each little chimney gained meant another thirty or forty vertical feet. We knew the mountain couldn't go on forever and at last stood at a spot where land again became mostly sky. A plaque, honoring Clarence King as the first director of the U.S. Geological Survey, marked the highest point in Utah, although many peaks looked equally high. One tired climber just back from South Kings told us not to be fooled—Kings is clearly higher. He had been fooled. From up here we could see a cluster of peaks all over 13,000 feet, including South Kings, Gilbert, Emmons, and Red Knob. The high, snowy, cone-shaped summit called Tokewanna Peak, at 13,123 feet, gleamed in the distance. When Mark arrived at the top, he stretched out on a flat boulder of the turtle's back and took a nice nap as though he rested on a hammock in his own backyard. Perhaps that was the highest nap he had ever taken, and the most enjoyable, judging from the smile on his face. This hour on the rugged, jagged summit made for pure mountaineity.

A new alpine melody started brewing for us. To the west, Tokewanna Peak darkened with bolts of lightning thrashing its flanks. Distant thunder awakened Mark, and we three descended rather quickly over loose slab, wobbly rocks, slippery snow, and rocking boulders. Another storm brewed to the south toward Vernal, with prehistoric forks of lightning stabbing the sky. But overhead, strangely enough, it remained clear and sunny. Arriving at Anderson Pass, our knees felt wobbly; even Willy, some twenty years younger, sat down for a rest just above the snowfield. Still, going down seemed quicker and easier.

We hopped and skipped down the snowfield we had so gingerly stepped up hours ago. I wished I had a pair of skis to swoosh down like an eagle to the little snow buttercups just blooming at the snowy base. Melting snow rolled in torrents down our trail, forcing us to skim the tops of boulders to the side. Pipits and rosy finches pursued their insect prey, sometimes almost brushing our shoulders. Thunder boomed to the south and west, but it looked like we would remain storm-free as the clouds sliced away from us. Meanwhile, Willy clicked away, busier than a cat chasing a butterfly.

At last we descended into the sunny meadow below Gunsight Pass. I managed to slip and catch myself with my hands as I fell sharply to the stony earth. A few drops of blood ran from the palm of my hand, reddening the already red Uintas. It felt good to soak my hand in a cold stream and press some watercress against the scratch. We stopped to chat with some campers in the high meadow who wondered how long it would take to get up to the top of Kings the next day.

"A lot easier than from Dollar Lake," we said.

Then came our ascent back up to Gunsight Pass. This was hard work after climbing Kings—so hard that I rested every hundred yards until I found a snowbank free of red algae. I quickly brushed aside the dirty surface to get down to a pure white inner layer and made myself a snow cone containing some harder hail pellets; quickly my energy returned.

"I hope you got a few pieces of magic, Willy."

"Yeah, I think so, but you know what Ansel Adams said—negatives are only the beginning. They are the musical score, but making the print is the performance of that score. I got a lot of work ahead of me. There are lots of things you can do to enhance a print in a darkroom, to highlight a shining flower in the sun." By six o'clock in the evening we had Gunsight Pass behind us as we plodded along the trail through the tundra and krummholz to Dollar Lake, mosquitoes and all.

Noodles in Alfredo sauce never tasted better, and so, too, did slices of dark bread and dried apricots, apples, and peaches boiled to perfection. We used the fruit-flavored boiling water (once the fruit was gone) to make hot tea; this new camp-side invention proved to be superb, even with an occasional mosquito.

Dollar Lake's waters soon reflected the moon, and three weary guys turned in for the night. I guess I dreamed of a ghost dance and woke up startled in the middle of the night. Echoing off the cliff sides of our valley came the eery, loud, high-pitched bugling of several elk. I listened for a few minutes and dozed off into a deep sleep in the high Uintas, an ancient continent within a continent, west-running though it was. The next morning we all felt a touch of sadness as we shouldered our heavy packs for our descent to the valley below.

Part II — False Summits of Mount Elbert

The three of us—Mark Reames, my son Rich, and I—got out of work too late to set up camp at Half Moon Creek later that night. Instead, we bunked at a motel in Leadville two miles above sea level. Winds whipped the streets of Leadville that September evening, forcing us to make a quick retreat to our room. We spread out a map of the Mount Elbert region and looked for the dotted line of the trail that led to the second highest peak in the lower forty-eight states. At 14,433 feet, Mount Elbert is only sixty-one feet lower than Mount Whitney in California. Our trail would merge for a short while with the Colorado Trail, which skirted the Rockies from Wyoming to New Mexico. It was too cold even inside the motel to stay up too long looking at maps, and we turned in to sleep soundly until 6 a.m.

The morning of September 11 proved to be fantastically clear—so clear that Leadville looked as though it would be swallowed up by the lurking summits of Mounts Elbert and Massive, laced in snow. By 8 a.m. we had our packs on and were proceeding at a rapid pace on the trail above Half Moon Creek Campground. Drooping aspen had already turned in color to a light yellow. Their leaves rustled with each gentle breeze. The usual suspects of Canada jays and Clark's nutcrackers squawked as we trudged by. Within an hour we reached tree line at 11,500 feet. But it was so chilly, we retreated to a clump of dwarfed spruce to put on sweaters and parkas and eat a bit of trail mix followed by swigs of water.

We proceeded more slowly out onto the windswept tundra, noticing that the late summer sunflowers had wilted to the ground. In fact, the entire grassy tundra appeared rust-colored in contrast with the greener ranch lands below. We thought we spotted the summit looming far above and slowed our pace down a bit more now that we had reached the 13,000-foot level. Rich pointed to the valleys below, with golden and glowing aspen groves looking like tongues of fire in narrow valleys. We had to keep moving in this brisk, chilly air. After a half hour or so of huffing and puffing, we reached what we thought was the summit, only to see yet more summits rising in the distance. Somehow this discouragement slowed me down all the more. In fact,

I stopped and rested more than usual. After a few swigs of canteen water, I proceeded snaillike up over windswept, rocky crests. We trekked along a more level spot but at an altitude higher than the summit of Longs Peak. Breathing became a bit difficult. My son, more than thirty years younger, decided to forge ahead and wait for us somewhere way up there.

Mark and I slowed down considerably as we crossed a fresh snowfield ankle-deep. At 14,300 feet, we stopped and rested. Neither of us had been this high before. The mountain seemed to be freaking me out. At last, we saw a second higher hump and an even higher summit crested with snow and people all gathered around looking like tiny grasshoppers. The hike from the second false summit to the true summit above 14,400 feet reminded me of the final approach to Kings Peak, with its nice, sheer views down into a bald glacial bowl to the west.

At last we met Rich at the true summit, where he had been waiting anxiously for us for forty-five minutes. We signed the register and sat down behind some rocks out of the wind to snack on oranges, rice cakes, and, of all things, fresh tomatoes from Mark's garden. We sprinkled them with salt and ate them voraciously, as though they were our first ever. A fat golden-mantled ground squirrel pestered Rich for food and took an apple core right out of his hand. We stood up again to stare into space—a fantastic view to the south past icy La Plata Peak to the Sangre de Cristo Range. To our west, the incredibly white Snowmass Peak and sheer-faced Capitol Peak. To the east and north, Pikes Peak and Longs Peak, both several hundred feet lower. We took one last glance around and ambled back down, hoping our knees wouldn't give out on a very steep descent, all the way back to Half Moon Creek Campground in a different world so far below.

Part III — Ascent to Infinity

Imagine a black volcano fleeced with snow clouds that clear momentarily to reveal three jagged peaks as white as Antarctica. Imagine those clouds spreading eastward in an early June sky to shed rain on a young corn crop of a Hopi mesa. This range, known as the

San Francisco Peaks of northern Arizona, has a mystical air about it, and for that reason alone we wished to climb it. The Hopi people of Arizona believe that ancient kachina spirits reside atop the San Francisco Peaks for a portion of the year. During the summer, the spirits become rain clouds and spread out from the mountain to three of their mesas in the desert. These life-giving clouds help corn mature to furnish food for both body and spirit throughout the rest of the year. The Hopi believe that when you eat corn, you can intuit the story of their existence. The mountain is clearly a sacred part of that story, as are kachina spirits (more than 160 different ones), which teach human beings the art of desert survival.

Three of us left Denver in late May by way of New Mexico to Flagstaff, Arizona. We hoped it would not be too early to attempt an ascent of the 4-million-year-old volcano's summit, which rises to the highest point in Arizona at 12,633 feet. We knew there would be snow, judging from the amount of shiny white stuff on the Sangre de Cristos of northern New Mexico; we sensed that it might even be tough going. But we were determined—so determined that we prepared ourselves with practice climbs of three other mountains before setting out on the Kachina Wilderness Trail outside Flagstaff.

Spending our first night in a friend's adobe home in the heart of the desert south of Santa Fe, we soon found ourselves bouncing along a forest service road going up Grandmother Spider Mountain (Tse-pi' na—Taylor Mountain) near Grants, New Mexico. Arriving on a high, windy plateau, Willy Sutton, Mark Reames, and I took swigs of water, shouldered our packs, and quickly paced along an ascending trail through groves of aspen mixed with Douglas fir. The trail underfoot was soft.

Laguna Pueblo author Leslie Marmon Silko refers to this mountain numerous times in her writings, particularly in her novel *Ceremony*. She has this to say about it: "She (Grandmother Spider) waited in certain locations for people to come to her for help. She alone had known how to outsmart the malicious mountain Kat'sina who imprisoned rain clouds in the northwest room of his magical house...." The spider had told an ancient mythical figure "Sun Man how to win the storm clouds back ... so they would be free again to bring rain and snow to the people." The spider for southwestern tribes is sacred. She taught humans the principle of weaving, whether carpet or story. For that matter, all animals have something to teach us, be they coyotes looking over their shoulders in caution, or two or three ants sharing the burden of carrying food with their strong-as-iron mandibles, or beavers thumping a warning with their tail when a tree they have chiseled is about to fall.

But to return to our trail—we emerged from the groves of aspen and fir onto slanting fields of grassy clumps that had the feel and look of Irish thatched cottages. The *malpais* (bad country) of dark lava fanned out on the valley floor below, glistening in the sun as though it was still steaming a thousand years ago. Grandmother Spider Mountain last erupted perhaps a million years ago in Mount St. Helens' fashion—blowing its stack out the side. Arms of lava (now covered with trees and grasses) finger outward from the peak like dark spider webs. Far above us lay snowfields tucked in the flank of the peak. We paused to watch a mountain bluebird flutter above the grasses, lending itself as a patch of blue to an otherwise cloudy sky. Chickadees sang out from a fringe of pine as we crisscrossed the grassy hummocks. We had the sensation of walking inside a landscape painting of Paul Cezanne set at 11,000 feet. Thunderheads built up to the west toward the Arizona line as we approached the base of the snowfield that rose some thirty feet to the peak itself. Perhaps Grandmother Spider was up to her old tricks again of liberating clouds from the trickster Kat'sina.

Since the snow lay at a steep pitch, we opted for an exposed rocky crevice, and in five minutes, we stood atop the spider's cephalothorax with spinnerets of elk sedge, currant bushes, and Indian rice grass. From up here at 11,600 feet, we could see a third of the state of New Mexico with most of the Pueblo villages for which this sacred spider means so much—a great rain cloud collector. Silko's Laguna Pueblo lay east-southeast. Acoma Pueblo, home of the Native American author Simon Ortiz, loomed southward. Santa Clara Pueblo, home of Maria the potter, stood to the northeast in the Rio Grande Valley. And far to the south lay N. Scott Momaday's Jemez Pueblo, setting for *House Made of Dawn* and some passages in *The Way to Rainy Mountain*. To our immediate north rose a spruce hummock. The smaller trees grew at the outer edges and the taller, wind-protected trees in the middle, similar to the forests of the savannah in the American Southeast. A steady wind buffeted us from an oncoming storm.

Webs of clouds began to collect in the lower valleys, and as the clouds from Arizona closed in, we could readily imagine our spider mountain catching some thunderheads. In *Ceremony*, Silko describes Tse-pi'na as "spinning out of the thunderclouds like gray spider webs and tangling against the foothills of the mountain." Scott Momaday writes in *The Way to Rainy Mountain* that:

> In New Mexico the land is made of many colors.
> When I was a boy I rode out over the red and
> Yellow and purple earth west of Jemez
> Pueblo ... I know what it is, on a hot day in
> August or September, to ride into a bank of cold,
> Fresh rain.

We, too, rode into a bank of cold rain as we rolled along eastern Arizona highways, leaving Tse-pi'na far behind.

We arranged for a rendezvous with two friends from Pennsylvania to climb the San Francisco Peaks, but after talking with them on the phone at a pit stop, we became a bit discouraged. They informed us that a freak blizzard had dumped four feet of fresh snow, trapping some climbers high up on Humphrey's Peak, the tallest of the San Francisco Peaks. Rescue parties succeeded in getting all stranded people off the mountain. Should we dare try it? "Let's meet anyway at the Snow Bowl Trailhead tomorrow," I told Gordon and Walt Fader. Thirty-four years earlier, Gordon and I had relived Henry David Thoreau's adventure by climbing Mount Katahdin above the black spruce forests of northern Maine.

We picked a camping spot under the Strawberry Volcano, which flanked the northeast slope of the very snowy San Francisco Peaks. Was the fresh snow really four feet deep? How deep was the older snow underneath? More clouds gathered that evening, looking like Chinese lanterns all lit up with thrashing heat lightning. A bit ominous, I thought to myself; we all read each other's mind. Thunder rattled in the distance like drums at some kachina ceremony. One last beer by the cozy campfire and we turned in, encouraged by the appearance of a star or two.

About four in the morning, a colony of coyotes yelped, but it was too early to get up. I went back into a deep sleep until a little before five-thirty. The coyotes were still yelping on a clear and glorious morning. Breakfast wolfed down, we headed for Strawberry Volcano to get in a little practice before ascending the Kachina Spirits Peak with the Faders or by ourselves the following day. Not a cloud in the sky—except for wisps around upper snowfields. Strawberry Volcano loomed above us the opposite way, with black and red cinders touching the sky. Mark Reames and I, who had both lived in Japan, couldn't help but think of Fuji San with all that black, pebbly ash spewed out from the lip of the crater. Willy was already racing up the steep slope a hundred yards ahead of us. Bright-green cabbagelike plants grew right out of the lava ash all the way upslope, looking just like a Georgia O'Keeffe painting. There's something about the desert that gets you. It's a kind of outer space on Earth. Green plants, black soil, red lava, blue sky, and a touch of white cloud make for stark austerity. Amid the volcanic starkness, we at last stood atop the rim of Strawberry Volcano.

It, too, had exploded out its eastward side several thousand years ago, leaving a crescent to face the rising sun. But within the crescent stood a half dozen Anasazi dwellings made of red blocks of lava. Since this volcano remained active until a thousand years ago, these ancient people lived within earshot of hissing steam vents. Down lower, they built retainer walls for rich black earth in which to grow yellow squash, white and red corn, and golden melons. How fantastic a village it must have been under a strong sun or a starry array with flickering, open-pit fires. Our hearts sensed the drumbeat.

The rising sun's rays glinted brightly off these Anasazi ruins, giving them a life of their own and extending their spirits into our tired century. The coyotes continued to yip-yap in the distance. Their presence in the Old West certainly engendered many a story. There is an old Hispanic legend about a Señor Coyote, and it goes like this. A rattler had a huge boulder fall on him while he was napping, but fortunately for the snake, a rabbit hopped by. He begged the rabbit to free him from the boulder. The rabbit complied, only to have the liberated snake announce that the rabbit would be his dinner for the day. However, Señor Coyote came along and the rabbit appealed to him for justice. The snake defended himself by saying that the rabbit had rolled the boulder on him and certainly deserved to be eaten. The coyote pretended that it was too complicated for him to understand and that they should reenact the story. When the snake was safely under the rock again, crushed in pain, Señor Coyote said, "*Pues* (well then), I guess you're stuck and that must be your reward for trying to eat the rabbit after he had treated you with such kindness."

It was now 6:30 a.m. and time to dash down the scree, a feat accomplished in minutes. We didn't encounter any rattlers or rabbits but continued to hear coyotes as we left three sets of tracks in the cinders en route to rendezvous with the Faders. Gordon and Walt arrived at the Snow Bowl with worried looks on their faces. They definitely did not wish to hike up through waste-deep snow to be rescued by a med-evac chopper. We had planned in advance to make the ascent the following day and teased them a little about going up to investigate. We finally consented to climb a lesser mountain near Sedona called Wilson Mountain, named after some poor soul who was gobbled alive by a grizzly bear in the last century.

Although there was no threat of snow, there was another hazard that didn't seem to bother the Faders. From their hiking information sheet, I quote:

HAZARDS—we do have various rattlesnake species throughout the area, so STAY ALERT! Coral snakes, also venomous, are listed for our area, mainly in the higher elevations (where we were going), but sightings are extremely rare. You are more apt to see a king snake (non-venomous but will bite), which is often mistaken for the coral snake—scorpions, centipedes, and black widow spiders may also be encountered ... Do not expose your hands, arms, or legs by placing them into spots where you can't see.

Sure beats snow!

We five put on our packs, filled our canteens, and marched out single file along a trail shimmering in heat. There wasn't the slightest trace of snow, but who knows? The beauty of this trail winding its way up Mount Wilson soon got to us. A pinyon jay scrambled through the clear air from pine branch to juniper shrub upslope, leading our eyes toward jagged red pinnacles of dark and lighter sandstone mixed with very dark bands of basalt glaring in the sun.

Numerous century plants, the first I'd ever seen, punctuated the brown hills with sixteen-foot stalks weighted down with bright red buds that were about to burst open into white blossoms—an event that occurs infrequently, perhaps once every hundred years. We were lucky. Heavily podded yucca plants scattered themselves on the open ground in and around the century plants. Desert tribes not only admired the beauty of the yucca plant, but also made use of it for sandals from its fibrous roots. They made soap from the yucca's roots mixed with water, fruit from its pods, necklaces from its black seeds, and food from the youngest tender roots, which taste something like a strong carrot.

No snakes or spiders so far, and definitely no snow. But we were thirsty. Consequently, we often paused to take a drink and sprinkle water on our heads. "We could have been in waist-deep snow," I said to Gordon with a twinkle in my eye. He (we) looked mighty hot, but we were gaining altitude and catching the faintest breeze from the wooded ridges above. A melodious Townsend's warbler trilled through the pinnacled canyons around us, but we could not echolocate him. Soon we stood on a ledge where earth met sky and moths met the yellow blossoms of knee-high prickly pear cactus. By now, a few shrubs of serviceberry graced the trailside, along with manzanita bushes that had crabapple-sized fruit, sometimes green, sometimes with a blush of red. Breeze or no breeze, it remained mighty hot, and I had to take a few swallows more of tepid canteen water.

"Let's try and make it to that saddle above for lunch," Mark suggested. We all grunted our consent and trudged several hundred feet higher until at last we rested our bones on light-green, lichen-covered rocks. We all simultaneously grabbed some oranges that were stowed in our backpacks; we peeled our oranges faster than a rattler's strike and savored each juicy morsel. Willy, with half an orange in his mouth, began to take black-and-white photos of the stark landscapes below the saddle. Above rose massive Wilson Mountain, silhouetted by stalks of red pods that rose ridiculously high above the century plant. Time for cheese and jalapeño-pepper bread, but not too much with my limited water supply.

"Hey, Willy—here's something you should photograph," we said, pointing to Wilson Mountain from behind a century plant.

"You don't take setups like that," Willy said. "Otherwise you're taking pictures of your own ideas. Too much is happening out there for you to bother with setups. You gotta let things happen."

He did take a shot of Wilson Mountain, but just as a cloud shadow touched its surface.

We raised our weary bones and proceeded along the trail into a mixed aspen–Douglas fir forest. It started to rain. It cooled us and we felt good. As the mist rose from the warm forest floor, I imagined I was in Rwanda looking for gorillas in the bush. Jays squawked in the temporary rain forest of Arizona. In the deep woods, just below the summit, we spotted a rufus-sided towhee and heard the high-pitched cheep of the bush tit. I really liked this gently rising forest. Manzanita bushes grew everywhere, and even wild strawberries.

The top of Wilson Mountain was flat—very flat. We hoofed through pleasing woods but looked for a break in the trees to get a view. We plodded onward until Walt Fader, running on ahead, found the trail's terminus. He stood in the distance, staring. No wonder. When we arrived at the edge of the cliff, all we could do was look down to endless gargoyles of colored sandstone. Two ravens followed the thermals in front of us. Vincent van Gogh would have gone mad here. The heck with cornfields and crows in Arles! Meanwhile, we had our own artist going mad. Willy did an Apache mountain spirits dance within our midst, clicking his camera everywhere—not anywhere, but everywhere suitable. We took mental snapshots of the kind that won't fade, especially of the manzanita bush in pink bloom perched at the dizzy edge of an 800-foot dropoff into a pink sandstone infinity.

Thunder rumbled, and we moved on to another part of the mountain, facing north and away from the storm to gaze at the distant and ever-so-white San Francisco Peaks (Nuvatukyaovi, or home of the kachina spirits) and tomorrow's climb. We could see that this mountain also blew its stack from the side in Mount Saint Helens' fashion, but 2 million years ago. Western meadowlarks and song sparrows spewed out rich pieces of dissolved landscapes with their melodious notes, flavored with yucca and sage. In bright sun, we stretched out for a bit of a nap, not worrying one iota about venomous coral snakes. Why should we worry, with their reputation of being seldom seen? However—lucky me—when I rolled in my sleepiness, I felt the sudden sting of a fang against my left knee. Fortunately, it was only a yucca plant. Nonetheless, my knee throbbed as much as if it had been a snakebite. By the time we had made our descent to the heat of the lower vales, my knee no longer hurt and my spirit soared in the company of my friends amid the stark desert landscape. It was sad to see the hand-waving Faders fade into the distance, making the present reality seem like a dream. Had we really climbed a mountain with them?

We camped that night on a high, windy flank of an inner basin, a deep valley within the volcanic caldera of the San Francisco Peaks. Under a moonless sky we dozed off, listening to the wind in the pines. I dreamed of my daughter's new apartment in Hoboken, New Jersey. I was still lugging furniture up ten flights of stairs, thinking how this would be good practice for climbing the highest peaks in Arizona. I looked out my daughter's window up on the fifth floor to see patches of green sycamore trees amid rows of brownstone apartments and shops. Somewhere out there was Nelson's Marine Bar, where a desert rat named Edward Abbey hung out between his lengthy stays in the canyonlands of Utah. Where in the world is Nelson's Marine Bar....

"Rise and shine," Willy shouted. "Coffee's on!" Somehow it had become early morning and time to get moving.

By 7 a.m. we stood at the Sun Bowl Trailhead, looking up at an incredibly white Humphrey's Peak, highest of the volcanic pinnacles. The sky was an intense blue with just a few wisps of clouds billowing over icy snowfields. It looked like the snow dropped well down into the upper forests—how far down we couldn't quite tell. Written on yesterday's register (May 31, 1992) was a message from a German climbing party that was simple and clear: "Snow too deep—had to turn around."

"But that was yesterday," said Mark with a gleam in his eye. We secured our packs and ambled at a comfortable pace through sweet-smelling, peaceful aspen groves. The creamy white trunks rose thick and straight. The branches quaked with myriad trembling leaves that looked like quivering feathers on a kachina dancer. The upper canopy of this aspen grove turned the sunlight green. No snow yet! Our gentle trail slowly zigzagged skyward, and aspen gave way to Douglas fir. Westerly vistas spread before us, revealing dozens of inactive volcanic humps. You'd think at least one of them would still be active, but nary a one. Trekking onward through columns of fir and pine, we began to feel the spirit of this mountain tug at us as rain clouds spread eastward toward the three Hopi mesas.

I remember once buying a beautiful free-standing hummingbird kachina doll (blossom fertilizer) in a pawnshop in Casper, Wyoming. It was an old doll, as the cottonwood root from which it was carved was splitting, and its green, bearded ruff had faded considerably. Because it was freestanding, it must have been made around 1950 or earlier. This doll, like many others, somehow got sold in the market instead of being burnt up to ashes, as it should have been. These colorful wooden dolls were once used solely as teaching devices, and once the Hopi child learned which kachina spirit this particular doll represented, the doll was destroyed by fire. I had this marvelous doll as part of my collection from 1976 until we moved to an apartment in Denver in 1990, when it, along with others, was stolen. At first I was mortified that I could no longer claim this unique spiritual curiosity as mine. Upon reflection, I realized how foolish I was to assume that this kachina doll was mine and only mine; I knew all along it should have been destroyed, because it had served its purpose as a wooden symbol of a powerful spirit. Thank you, whoever you are, for separating me from this most touchable replica.

Erna Fergusson described Hopi dancers getting ready early in the morning for imploring kachina spirits to bring rain clouds:

> Peering over the rocks, we could see the dancers gathered on a flat stretch of sand sheltered by an overhanging rock. They were already dressed in dance kirtles and sashes, fringed brown moccasins, and flaring shirts of pinyon boughs. Their bodies were smeared with corn-smut, a sort of dare to the gods to send rain and wash it off. On each torso were interlocking crescents done in white paint, symbols of friendship. The gaudy masks sat in a row on the rocks, waiting and looking curiously human.

By now, at 9,000 feet or so, we encountered our first small patches of snow. They got deeper when the trail passed through ravines. Just on the upper side of one of these ravines, we paused for some water and a little trail mix. A young woman from Phoenix stopped to chat, saying that she had never before encountered so much snow this late in the season (it was only June 1, and no Colorado mountain worth its salt could be climbed this early without winter gear). She asked if it was okay to accompany us, and the four of us climbed merrily in the deepening snow until we came to a lava flow, where the trail seemed to end. The girl waited while we proceeded to climb the green, lichen-covered lava to look for the continuation of the trail. No luck. What happened to it? The girl shouted that she had discovered the switchback was right where she sat, and that we all had missed it. She went on with another climbing party while we gingerly descended the wobbly lava flow, all the while looking at the quaking aspen forests far below.

Erna Fergusson wrote:

> As the dancers climbed over the rocks, we saw first the feathers and spires of headed grass which topped the masks. Each mask is in itself a cloud symbol and bears many symbols

of cloud and rain and a rainbow on its terraced top. At the back of each one a small Kachina doll stood on a carved ear of corn or on another Kachina. Around the neck was a ruff of spruce, a Kachina symbol, and each man carried spruce in one hand, the inevitable rattle in the other. Jingling and talking, they appeared, first the gay-colored masks, then the men, a long line. They stopped a moment at a shrine built of slabs of rock, added their quota of meal to the white scatterings already there, and then moved on across the causeway.

Clouds gathered in from the west, but they were not the least bit threatening. The snow deepened among aisles of spruce, and the Phoenix girl was on her way back. "Too much snow," she said, "but keep on following the tracks to the right. The couple I was with is determined to make it." Sometimes we sank up to our knees in fresh and glistening snow, but for the most part, the three of us carefully edged our way skyward. At one point, the trail of footprints went straight upslope, with no zigzags. This proved to be tiresome above 10,000 feet, especially when you didn't know if you would break through snow and sink up to your hips.

Fergusson poetically continued:

The maskers danced first in the narrow plaza in front of the first house in Walpi. The first movement was simple: rhythmic pounding of the feet in perfect time, as the bodies swing now right, now left, showing front and back views of the weird masks, the swishing skirts. All the time dancers sang, catching without error the frequent changes of tempo. To and fro they swung, to and fro, following the leader's chant, intoning the deep droning prayer, curiously muffled under the masks.

At the top of this steep hill, we raised our canteens and gurgled cold water down our dry gullets and ate a handful of trail mix. We could begin to see the Snow Bowl Ski Area to our right and heard and finally saw a three-toed woodpecker jackhammering a dead spruce in search of insects. A chickaree squirrel chattered upslope somewhere, and ravens flew overhead, convincing us of the fitness of the name "San Francisco Peaks" in honor of the twelfth-century Saint Francis of Assisi, who loved animals of all kinds. St. Francis wrote a charming small volume called *Little Flowers*, in which he recorded his tender words for turtle doves, which he prevented from being sold as food: "O my little sisters, simple, innocent, pure doves, why have you let yourselves be caught? Now I wish to save you from death and make nests for you, so that you can be fruitful and multiply as God your Maker ordained." This mountain wilderness remains a perpetual nest for wildlife.

Our trail of scant footprints led to the northern edge of the Snow Bowl (not part of the wilderness area), where we caught our first glimpse of wintry Agassiz Peak, rising above like one of the Himalayas. Would we ever make it? Some of us began to have secret doubts. God, it was a long ways up there. At last we came to the couple who had made tracks ahead of us. "This is it," they said. "The snow has completely obliterated the trail and the snow is soft." But there was another option—a loose volcanic scree served as a pathway to the sky. "I know what yer thinkin'," one of the climbers said. "But that stuff is loose as hell. I wouldn't try it if I were you." But that was like speaking to a stone wall (no pun intended). We had to do it—that's why we came here. We just had to do it.

Erna Fergusson wrote:

> Then they stopped and stood at ease while the leaders prepared for the second movement. First they arranged on the ground a row of folded blankets, dirty quilts, whatever they had or whatever women threw down from the housetops. On these the seven women figures knelt, facing the men. In front of each woman was a hollow gourd, and each one wielded the deer-scapula to bring out a hollow squawking, so perfect in rhythm as not to be unpleasant. Chanting, the Kachinas danced to this music, the steps a little more vigorous than in the first figure.

We three began our scramble up loose scree. It was so black that hardly any snow remained, so strong was the June sun. At first it seemed like fun, but after a half hour or so of losing our footing, sliding backward every time we pushed forward, and seeing very little progress in total elevation gained, we realized we were in for some difficult work. Sometimes harder ledges of lava gave us firmer footholds and handholds, and sometimes we had to cross loose volcanic gravel which put everything into slow motion, as in a dream. The snowy forest that skirted the edge of the lava flow gradually thinned out to mere dwarfs. We could no longer spot the two climbers below, as everything merged with the gigantic Snow Bowl and Agassiz Peak.

Now halfway up to the lip of the volcano, we paused (each at a different level in space) to take a drink of cool water. Just as I stood up to forge onward, two air force jets buzzed the edge of the volcanic rim no more than a thousand feet above us, their thunderous roar frightening us and causing us almost to lose our footing. My first reaction of fear rapidly transformed to anger. Was not this sacred mountain part of the Kachina Wilderness Area? Is there not a sufficient number of other lesser volcanoes the jets could buzz? Why buzz a wilderness area? Congress must see to it that wilderness areas be left in peace and not be abused by military jets. Such practice must cease.

The Wilderness Act of 1964, signed by President Lyndon Johnson, states:

> A designated wilderness is an area of underdeveloped Federal land set aside by Congress and administered for the enjoyment of the public, scientific research, scenic and historic values. This is accomplished in a manner so as to leave it unimpaired for future generations. More specifically, we define wilderness as a relatively large natural area that is neither easily accessible nor frequented by motorized vehicles. The wilderness is an area where opportunities exist for primitive types of recreation; where past and current human activities are not readily apparent.

So states the forest service handout entitled "The Kachina Peaks—Inner Basin Wilderness Guide." A military jet is a motorized vehicle that impairs the enjoyment of the public.

The upper third of the lava flow proved to be less tiresome than the first section just above the trail. In fact, at timberline or a little below, we picked up the trail once again, which wound its way through hummocks of bristlecone pines that were all twisted, windswept, and gnarled. Patches of snow, sometimes three feet deep, occasionally obscured the trail. Agassiz Peak, named after the Swiss glaciologist whose theories inspired young John Muir to develop his own glacial theories of Yosemite, rose above, but now more as a high hump than a foreboding Himalayan peak. A symphony of white-crowned sparrows and hermit thrushes piped from the valleys below.

Willy was the first to make it to the lip of the volcanic crater. From down below it looked like he was doing a kachina spirits dance. Mark was next, and then I came trudging along to a spot where I could see out into the desert toward the three Hopi mesas in direct path of the clouds. Erna Fergusson described the climax of the kachina spirits dance at Walpi:

> Finally the priests signaled for the end, sprinkled meal to indicate the line of march, and led their troupe to the second plaza. There the figures were repeated in front of the Snake Rock, where for this occasion a small spruce tree had been planted and decorated with a few floating breath feathers. The priests, as they scattered meal upon the dancers, threw pinches of it also at the tree. The dance was the same. A few more spectators had gathered. A woman, following the priests, quietly threw meal on all the dancers, especially upon the kneeling women figures, whose wigs were becoming well powdered with it. Then the whole party moved to the western plaza.

The dance was over. But our dance was just beginning. Willy continued on to a higher knob, hopping around with camera in hand. Mark and I scampered around a lesser San Francisco Peak below Humphreys that was layered with deep snow. It was not quite as high as Agassiz but was higher than Fremont Peak. Because there was so much snow, we could not see a species of groundsel called *Senecio franciscanus*, a yellow-flowered tundra plant found nowhere else in the world. To our east stretched the Inner Basin (caused by the sideways explosion 2 million years ago), with cascades of avalanched snow tumbled on top of older snow, reminiscent of riptide patterns of the New Jersey shore not far from my daughter's place. Tired though we were, we hopped from rock to rock to gain a different perspective. The forests and springs of the Inner Basin looked as inviting as Shangri-la. Light green aspen leaves blended with the darker pine and spruce just below the snow line. It was easy to see how this mountain could generate its own weather to send rain clouds eastward.

"Well, whatya think we should say or do up here on this sacred mountain?" Mark inquired of Willy and me as we ate oranges and trail mix.

"Let's just say a wee prayer for a good corn rain," I suggested. We three remained silent for a moment or two. The air up here was supercharged with energy, and although our bodies were weary, we remained just as alert, alive, and excited as we had been at the bottom of the mountain.

Since the hour of three rapidly approached and we had lots of snow to negotiate, it was time for us to dance downward. But we never left that peak in a sense. Part of our spirits remains up there being infinitely energized.

PART IV — TWO MEN AND A DOG ATOP MOUNT WHEELER

For a reprieve from graduate studies at the University of New Mexico, my wife Maura and I used to visit the Taos Pueblo nestled beneath snowy Mount Wheeler. One time, we struck up a conversation with a tribal elder who was a member of the tribal council. He said, "Will you look up there at old Mount Wheeler? It's sure sticking up there against the blue sky, isn't it?" When I asked him if he had ever climbed Wheeler, the highest peak in New Mexico, he said that he had done so, many times. "Way up there," he said with a chuckle, "there's a spring that remains so cold in the middle of summer that it almost hurts you to drink from it. But I always stop there for a drink." He suggested that we climb it once summer returned. I didn't get around to climbing Mount Wheeler until some thirty-three years later in the year 2000.

My friend Jonny Boucher of Mount Katahdin and Halla San days came across from England for a short stay in early September. We had decided to climb this mountain despite stern warnings he had received from a dignified, gray-haired British lady, his neighbor, that he surely must realize that this Mount Wheeler stood in the midst of a forbidding desert! We brought along with us my little blond cocker spaniel Mini, who had ascended three fourteeners and eight other thirteeners with me in times past. Although she was born in Summerville, South Carolina, she took to the Colorado tundra like salmon to the Copper River. In Denver, Jonny and I checked trail maps of the Kit Carson National Forest and Mount Wheeler while Mini ate some dog-bone treats. We packed the car that night with camping and climbing supplies and all turned in early.

Arriving at a Rio Hondo campsite near the Taos Ski Area, we set up our tent, fed Mini, and ate fire-cooked steaks and potatoes. We then proceeded to the trailhead for a twilight glimpse of our climb the next morning. Mini wanted to climb the mountain right then and there. It proved to be an extremely chilly night for early September, and when Mini whimpered in the middle of the night, I opened up my sleeping bag so she could crawl in for extra warmth. Once, in the middle of the night, she got up and crawled in with Jonny, who was simply delighted.

At dawn, we three hopped out of the tent and into the even colder air, our breaths all steaming. Fire lit, we felt a bit warmer, and after we swilled hot coffee, we felt even better. As Mini danced around the fire with an occasional bark for a scrap of food, we stuffed our day packs with energy bars and water and soon hit the trail. Mini, of course, led the way up through Douglas fir and lodgepole pines. Clusters of pink fireweed and pearly everlasting graced the edge of the woods. The trail steepened as we arrived at a small, stagnant pond, where the trail headed due south up a rocky escarpment that afforded us views of the Pecos Mountains and Taos Valley. We rested to chug some water and to spritz water into Mini's mouth. She wolfed down a cheddar-cheese cracker and raced ahead on the ever-upward trail. The sky remained azure blue, and by now the sun was warming things up quite a bit. Rugged hills to the southwest still loomed much higher than our elevation of around 10,000 feet.

Jonny and I reminisced about our climbs of the past: Katahdin, Halla San, and only two years earlier, Mount Princeton, just to the north of Tabeguache. For forty-two years, on and off, we had gotten together for a bit of mountaineering. Jonny's highest ascent was Mount Kilimanjaro, well over 19,400 feet. With a guide, it took him four days. Today's ascent would get us to the highest point in New Mexico, at 13,161 feet—slightly less than his ascent of Mount Kinabalu of 13,454 feet in Borneo, when he climbed from warm rain-forest jungles to downright chilly dwarf forests and frosty, damp tundra high above the South China Sea. Jonny had spent more than thirty years of his life in Asia as a bank officer for the Bank of Hong Kong–Shanghai and had devoted his spare time to climbing hills and mountains. But now, much later in our lives, we had a hard time keeping up with pacesetting Mini. She had a way of beckoning you onward with her sad brown eyes and wiggling stump of a tail.

At last we reached tree line and the beginning of a long hump of tundra. We could no longer spot the pronounced heights of Mount Wheeler, as we were able to do far below. Mini chased song sparrows up and down the bald hills, moving her little feet as quickly as the harpsichord notes of a Domenico Scarlatti sonata. She climbed the mountain thrice for our once. Her brown eyes sparkled with joy. Up here, sunflowers blew in breezes in an already browning tundra. Those high peaks to the southwest, including Jicarita Peak, no longer rose above us—they only equaled our elevation. Oh no, our trail began to descend! What's going on here? Should we freelance it over to a false summit to our south? To play it safe, we descended the switchbacks down into a krummholz forest of limber pines that were hissing in the wind. Here we sat down and ate some energy bars, which we shared with Mini, who then drank from a stream while we guzzled water from our bottles.

The sky remained clear as we stood up and commenced our hike through the twisted pines of tree line and straight up into the tundra. The trail showed no mercy as it led us up a fifty-degree slope toward an amazingly level bald ridge. We sixty-plus-year-olds huffed and puffed and rested while Mini dashed skyward like a ballerina doing pirouettes, only to bound back downslope to two human tortoises. She tried to speed us up, to no avail. But we finally stood atop a level ridge that led toward several false summits, with the rocky hump of Wheeler rising even higher. Below us lay the sacred Blue Lake of the Taos Pueblo, glistening like a jewel. It is here that certain secret ceremonial practices have been conducted by this tribe for centuries. President Nixon, in a surprise move, returned the Blue Lake to the Taos Pueblo midway through his first term. It should have never been severed from the Taos Pueblo to begin with. But there it lay, about 500 feet below us, crescent-shaped and nestled against the eastern slope of the Wheeler complex. We did see several human figures seated along its lakeshore; they were wrapped in colorful blankets.

Just before we started our climb of a false summit, I had shooting pains in my stomach. I had to rest. Poor Jonny thought he had come all the way from London, only to be stopped 300 vertical feet shy of our objective. But miraculously, my pain vanished and we proceeded slowly and cautiously up the false summit. You guessed it—Mini stood atop that little peak ten minutes or so before we trudged up to her level. Up here, slightly above 13,000 feet, there was no vegetation to speak of, only gleaming stones. We dropped back down to climb yet another lesser peak, with Wheeler rising just a bit higher. Those distant peaks to the southwest clearly lay at a significantly lower elevation. Our campsite valley looked impossibly far away, and in the distance, the table mesa of Taos and vast high deserts stretched westward. We could see wee specks of people atop Wheeler perhaps several hundred yards away.

Mini, with her long, floppy ears blowing in the wind, led the way to the summit, where several other dogs, much larger than Mini, accompanied their masters. We gazed all around a great circle of

New Mexico lying far below. The air was so clear we could see as far as the Arizona border, with the Grandmother Spider Mountain in between. We three sat down for a much-needed rest. We drank water and nibbled on cheddar-cheese crackers (which Mini loved) and dried apricots. Very sadly, within a week of our descent from this lofty summit and return trip to Denver, poor Mini died suddenly of autoimmune disease. Her ashes rest in our backyard under a marker on South York Street. I truly loved her as a special spirit of God's creation. For a South Carolina swamp dog, she took to the mountains like no other dog I have known. Jonny e-mailed me from London to share his grief. He called her a priceless little duchess of South York.

CHAPTER SIX

VIVA LOS PECOS Y LA SIERRA DE SAN JUAN

In Memory of Mark Reames

Part I — Los Pecos

They beckon all who gaze at their glistening banks of snow above blue-green skirts of forest. South Truchas Peak is New Mexico's third highest, at 13,102 feet. It dominates the Pecos Wilderness Area and the minds of people who come under its spell. These mountains have certainly engendered numerous mythic stories. One of them concerns greedy Spaniards in search of gold. A young Indian lad called Pin-ne-qua, who was susceptible to flattery, led forty Spaniards into the high mountains, where he had earlier stumbled across a vein of gold. Kiosh, the evil one who remains strong in the hearts of those who seek material wealth, immediately entered upon the scene. He changed the course of the sun, causing the gold seekers to trudge in the wrong direction. A thirst-crazed Spaniard killed Pin-ne-qua in a rage. Eventually, each and every thirsty soldier dropped to his death.

Not seeking gold and having plenty of water, Mark Reames and I packed into the Pecos Wilderness from the Santa Barbara Campground, where glittering evening stars had entranced us the night before. Now, pines glowed resinously in the morning sun. Forty shades of green raced up the mountainsides in the form of aspen, dwarf maple, squaw currant, and numerous other varieties of underbrush. Bursts of color punctuated the inclining trail: lavender shooting stars, blue-and-white columbines, purple iris, scarlet Indian paintbrush, sulphur flower, and clusters of golden banner. Perhaps Pin-ne-qua's vein of gold was really nothing more or less than golden banner. Imagine armor-plated Spaniards marching in columns to seize golden banner!

We sat for a rest in the depths of an aspen grove, serenaded by the ethereal notes of a Swainson's thrush, much like some distant Indian flute player. For us, the thrush matched the landscape, translating it with rare refinement. Its notes enter the spirit's core.

Our backpacks became more burdensome the higher we hiked. With this pack, I weighed more than 220 pounds and trudged much like an overly heavy man placing one foot firmly ahead and gliding the body forward as though walking were an engineering project. We took many rests. We took many swigs of water, thankful we were not Spanish soldiers being led by Pin-ne-qua. At times, the trail up the Middle Fork skirted the edge of the slope like a mountain goat's trail. When we arrived at a gently sloping meadow of skunk cabbage and tall grasses, we dispensed of our packs to scout out a campsite. Finding one by a trickling brook in a cathedral of tall white aspen, we set up camp with a ring of rocks for a fire and fallen logs for seats.

To the southwest rose the Barbara Divide, flanked with snow. Behind us, a densely forested slope of aspen, fir, and spruce rose up to the obscured Jicarita Peak. The roar of the Middle Fork River far below resonated pleasingly through the forest and meadow. I filled and purified a jug of water for cooking our meal and lit a campfire in the late afternoon sun. Thankfully, we had sufficient water and juice to quench our thirst.

As the sun sank below a western ridge, a bright crescent moon with its partner Jupiter appeared, and then the Big Dipper and Mars. Before long, the Way of Souls, or the Milky Way, glittered like a ceremonial sash across the sky. Ralph Waldo Emerson once wrote that if the stars had appeared but once in human history, it would have been recorded as a phenomenal, mythological event worthy of worship. Shooting stars dashed across the sky like tracer bullets. The temperature on this late June night started to drop, forcing us back to the fire and into our sleeping bags to watch the stars flicker and gleam until they became part of our dreams.

We awakened at 6:15 a.m. to a glorious, cloudless morning. Again, I lit a fire to kill the frost that had gathered around the campsite vegetation. Amazing to think meadow flowers could withstand such a burden each night! But they adjust somehow, just like humans adjust to the burden of heavy backpacks. Skies of stars and skies of sun help nurture these flowers to fullness of bloom.

After breakfast, we put hard-boiled eggs, candy bars, oranges, and cheese into day packs and made sure our canteens were filled to the brim. Our destination? Jicarita Peak, looming in the sky at 12,750 feet, flanked with deep snow on its eastern side. Notes from Swainson's thrushes and ruby-crowned kinglets lifted our spirits as we walked ever higher along the trail. The more elevation we gained, the smaller and less mature grew the skunk cabbage in even chillier air. We paused to listen to the high-pitched shrill of the whistle pig that scurried along the rocky exposures beneath the tundra. Why were there outcroppings of rock flows every now and then? Were they encouraged by destabilizing water seepage and underground springs? Rock flows streaked the mountain like strokes of gray in a Monet painting. Clusters of flag irises lent a pointillistic touch.

A raven cawed in the sky, refocusing our attention to alpine heights forever above in a blue dome of sky. We again quickly paced up through the tree line into a bald tundra. The usual pipits and rosy finches flicked through the air, warmed by the burning disk of radium up in the sky. Still there were no clouds. Within an hour we stood, at last, atop the Santa Barbara Divide to stare into New Mexican space far and near. Near our feet—delicate pink Parry primrose, white moss campion, and purple alpine forget-me-nots. Far away—the hazy depressions of Mora Valley and the flat eastern plains. There was a stiff alpine breeze, so we dropped below a protective ledge and snacked on our lunch of sky for the soul and food for the body. The sky defines western lands like no other region in America. Western clouds sometimes even replicate terraced landforms below, as though the land had urged the clouds to conformity. Nowhere else have I sensed planetary space stretching forever as I have here. The sky does feed the soul. We know we are part of the universe. It's as though we stood on some fresh and new planet that was light-years away.

We moved on toward the summit along a faint trail lined with blue sky pilots and yellow alpine avens. Skirting the flanks of an adjoining peak, we scrambled upward to the windiest spot in New Mexico—or so it seemed. Others thought so, anyway, as a high windbreak of rocks had been constructed to give climbers reprieve.

Lunch eaten, we ambled across the high summit of Jicarita Peak to its Taos side and gazed at New Mexico's highest peak, Mount Wheeler, 13,161 feet, and the ever-so-distant Wolf Creek Pass and the San Juans of Colorado, which we would explore in another season. All lay socked in snow and impossible to climb without winter gear and determination. Sunny Jicarita was a good choice indeed, despite the wind—but not just for distant views. Along came some bighorn sheep. They nudged closer and closer toward us, looking a bit like helmeted conquistadors. They came ridiculously close. Now we could see their soft brown eyes and the gray ridges of their curved horns. They reared up on their hind legs, pretending to challenge each other. I backed away. They followed. Along came a third ram. I became frightened. We both backed away, although Mark seemed less shy than I was. Clearly we had invaded their territory, and they simply moved us off the peak, herding us like sheep. We rapidly descended an angular snowfield while they stood holding their ground as kings of the mountain. We had come eyeball to eyeball with creatures that are much closer to the land than we are.

After another snack at the base of the snowfield, we waved goodbye to our brief acquaintances, who were still guarding the mountaintop, and descended quickly to the tree line filled with thrush and kinglet music. We soon stood at our peaceful campsite. Another campfire lit, we wolfed down hot stew and watched the sun sink into the western desert. The atmosphere glowed as golden as Spanish dreams. From stargazing to sleep to the next morning's light seemed like mere minutes.

I sipped with pleasure from my steaming mug of coffee as I stood amid frosty flowers. This third day in the backcountry of New Mexico proved to be cloudless, although a distant forest fire haze was visible to the west. Today we would go up a different draw to the Barbara Divide, closer to the snowy Truchas Peaks. Lunches in our packs, we crossed the Middle Fork Rapids on two shaky logs, one being slicker than grease. We then sprang up the trail lined with mossy spruce and entered an open meadow graced with a gentler stream that cut into banks with swirling pools—ideal for brook trout. Pin-ne-qua and his Spaniards should have come to these golden meadows. No sign of Kiosh, the evil one. Just butterflies and robins and endless flowers under a blue arch of sky.

Our trail steepened somewhat and we soon saw our first patch of snow. Before long, the snow wasn't in patches but in one continuous field, which deepened the higher we trudged. A foolish time for me to be in short pants! Sometimes I'd fall through the snow and scratch my legs on poking branches on the way down. It wasn't much fun getting back out. At times my scratches created their own watermelon snow—snow with a pink tinge. I was sorely tempted to head over to a soggy marsh laced with marsh marigolds and take my chances with mud rather than with snow, but I could see the clear tundra a few hundred yards ahead. A little higher up, the hardened snow gave us more support. We were thankful to step out onto the sunny, clear tundra under the turquoise heavens above. Sky thoughts prevailed. Isolated though the tundra is, loneliness is hardly a factor—too many sky pilots and alpine forget-me-nots.

Atop the divide we peered into space—hundreds of miles of pure space. To our west loomed the Truchas Peaks, which were well over 13,000 feet and as white as Moby Dick. To our east stretched the foothills and distant summit of Hermit Peak above Las Vegas,

New Mexico. To our north was yesterday's mountain guarded by rams. To our south, we saw the dim outline of Sandia Crest outside Albuquerque. Sandia Mountain's western face appears at sunset to be like a giant, split-open red watermelon—hence its Spanish name, "Sandia." I remember having tried to climb that peak in February some twenty-five years earlier. What appeared to be a mere dusting of snow on the bright-red, pinnacled crest of Sandia from far below proved to be tiring, waist-deep snow—so tiring, I was forced to turn around 800 feet shy of the jagged summit. Here on the Barbara Divide, tiny stones sparkled at my feet. Upon closer examination, I discovered not gold but quartzite arrow chippings from Pin-ne-qua's people, the ancient Pueblos. They, like the Spanish, must have enjoyed mutton, too, as these mountaintops are fairly sprinkled with quartzite points. A few of the arrows were made of dark obsidian, probably obtained through trade with the tribes of Mexico.

Descending, we avoided all the deep snow and took our chances with wet marshes, which led to lower, drier vales. Wet and soggy they were but equally flowerful with white marsh marigolds and yellow snow buttercups. Thrushes serenaded us. Distant waterfalls thundered. But we really had to find the trail once again. It meant climbing up through shallower snow all the while looking for footprints. Where were our footprints? As the sun dipped lower in the sky, I became apprehensive. I didn't want to sleep in snow or wet marshes. Where were our footprints? What if we crossed our old trail on slightly open ground where there were no prints? What if... and there they were—sets of melting holes in a foot of snow. A mile of this downhilling got us to scant patches and eventually the open, dusty trail.

It was good to bathe in a meadow stream below. The sun was strong enough to counteract the icy water. Butterflies fluttered and all the feathered gang sang. We would watch the stars that evening in the peace and security of our campsite. Going back down with less heavy packs to civilization was all that we had left to do. We had seized several days of our lives from the city to be in the peaks of the Pecos near and far.

Part II – La Sierra de San Juan

Dawn's first glimmer revealed the silver tones of subalpine firs. High peaks, looming above the Blue Lakes, began to glow like fragments of the moon brought closer to Earth. Today we would climb a 26-million-year-old volcanic spire known as Mount Sneffels in the San Juans of southwestern Colorado. Yesterday we had noticed its north-facing, angular snowfields above Ridgeway, but now, as I crawled out of the tent, it appeared naked and barren, yet alluring, so high it rose in an orange sky.

Back in 1874, when Frederic Endlich of the Hayden Expedition first cast his eyes on this jagged spire, he exclaimed, "There's Snaefel," referring to a fictional mountain in Jules Verne's *Journey to the Center of the Earth*. As we plodded along our trail 120 years later, I had the impression that I was on a journey to the center of the moon—a moon with flowers, that is. Along our way toward the upper Blue Lakes there bloomed a profusion of colorful flowers: ever-so-rosy paintbrush, blue columbine, purple larkspur, yellow alpine avens, red queen's crown, and pink moss campion. All of these soft and delicate plants fused with spires of rock in the sun. The basin echoed with the high-pitched squeaking of marmots and squawking ravens high in the sky. Now we could see across our lower basin from the top of the rolling tundra slopes, which reminded me of coastal Newfoundland, Canada. They were soft underfoot, just as I remembered from my thirty-day excursion to Newfoundland in 1958. The lower and upper Blue Lakes form a large volcanic caldera fringed with black and brown spires high in the sky. Soft tundra and volcanic rock marry to form a San Juan haiku of contrasting beauty.

It was peaceful walking along the shoreline of the third Blue Lake. We noted small circles form on the lake's surface, indicating the presence of trout. Our trail suddenly rose with zigzags upward like stitches on the side of a steep, dark ridge, at the top of which rested Blue Lake Pass. My son, Rich, led the way, with Mark Reames and me following. Sometimes the width of the trail occupied only a few inches of steep slope. One false move and you'd be history. Still the flowers grew among pinnacles of rock. All-white columbines graced one little rocky nook far above the wind-rippled Blue Lakes. At nighttime such flowers are iridescent even without the moon. Starlight is enough to give them a glow. Snowfields add to this effect. This is why, I believe, Frank Waters contends in his book *The Colorado* that the Rockies emit light all of their own in the dark of night.

Who can say how far my mind wandered off this steep and narrow trail, although my feet remained glued to it. Upward forever. My son and Mark momentarily disappeared—because they stood atop Blue Lakes Pass at 13,000 feet. And then came me. Yankee Boy Basin spread eastward, and that stubborn Mount Sneffels, with all sorts of jagged spires, rose forever above. One climber sat with his daughters sporting a handmade cane that had a curved hickory wood handle. It resembled an ice ax, although it was much lighter and more manageable. Another group of boisterous climbers from Kansas assembled below us, pondering their route up Sneffels from this pass via difficult spires, or back into Yankee Boy Basin and up a steep and rocky couloir. They didn't seem to pay any attention to a spritelike rosy finch hopping at their feet. Perhaps it had flown down from the summit in a moment's time. My climbing party elected to descend to the beginning of the couloir, but not without sitting and staring westward into a brown-peaked volcanic basin above our campground. We knew we would explore this trailless valley on another day when we hoped to have Sneffels behind us. We wanted to take the time to sit and listen to cascading rocks tumbling from peaks above, to collect a geode or two, to watch buck deer dance across the tundra, and finally to wash our faces late in the day in the icy spray of waterfalls.

But Sneffels had to be ascended before late afternoon thunderheads built up. It is no place to be with thrashing lightning and volcanic thunder. Down we plodded to the upper fields of Yankee Boy Basin, where once-adventuresome men mined silver and gold. Our silver and gold lay ahead of us in the form of adventure. Our necks hurt as we looked straight up this rocky, dusty couloir with antlike climbers hundreds of feet above. Step by step is the way—not to worry about how long it will take or how tired you will get. However, my boot tread was badly worn and I slipped backward too often for comfort. As my son and Mark climbed steadily above, I moved over to bigger rocks and things went better. I made time by grabbing one boulder after another until humans below appeared as ants. But there remained half a couloir above with tiny human heads peering over the edge at me and others. A rock from far above came loose and tumbled downhill, clinking and clanking and clacking along the way. French climbers shouted to each other, "*Faites attention, attention!*" They quickly moved out of the way as the rock fell harmlessly to the base without injury to anyone.

With hundreds more hand grabs and wobbly rocks underfoot, I made it to the lip of the couloir, where Mark stood all smiles. Rich had gone on up yet another narrow couloir to the summit. I followed Mark closely up a rockier, snowy couloir as Yankee Boy Basin unfolded below like a dream. We could see where a big boulder had torn loose, leaving a trail of chink marks and chips on lower rocks and ledges. A half hour later we arrived at the 14,000-foot lip of this narrow chute. Rich stood above us and waved. "This way," he said, as he pointed to a narrow chimney to our left. Up we shimmied and out onto a dirt and stone trail that led us to the top of the 14,150-foot crest of Mount Sneffels. With a third of Colorado spreading below, we stood and stared, barely controlling the grins on our faces atop the highest of surrounding spires in the sun.

POSTSCRIPT:

Just one week later, Mark Reames fell to his death in the mountains above Boulder, Colorado, on a relatively easy scramble across some rocky ledges. He was with his brother on his brother's birthday. The fact that it could have happened on Sneffels haunted both Rich and me for months. I treasure those moments in the sky with Mark. He was a true companion along many a trail.

CHAPTER SEVEN

A NEW ENGLAND INTERLUDE: THOREAU'S MONADNOCK

New England never looked greener. White pines towered over the village of Concord, Massachusetts, where I attended the annual Thoreau Society meeting in the intense heat of mid-July. The heat was so overbearing that I had difficulty listening to the various lectures. But one of the delightful escape options for attendees was a guided climb of Mount Monadnock, New Hampshire, including finding the spot where Thoreau spent several nights in August 1860.

Five of us, including a more subdued Ike Rodman (with whom we climbed Mount Bierstadt), set out for Keene, New Hampshire, on July 17 with our guide, José García, a professional botanist and immigrant from Cuba who moved to the United States after the Bay of Pigs Invasion in 1961. Hopping out of our van, we began our hike via the Spellman Trail through a dense mixed forest of paper birch, white pine, giant beech trees with heart-shaped leaves, and thick stands of hemlock. We walked along Henry David Thoreau's route of 1852, and in two short miles through fragrant forests, we gained 2,000 feet to arrive at Thoreau's favorite wild bog, piping with white-throated sparrows and eastern warblers. Thoreau wrote that these nice little bogs of Monadnock stayed perpetually moist by "retaining some of the clouds" that hovered above. José pointed out a surrounding canopy of striped maple (with very large leaves) and golden-barked yellow birch with a forest floor of New York ferns. The valleys of New Hampshire spread far below, and we could begin to make out the high, rocky shell of Monadnock, looking like a giant sleeping turtle whose shell rose above tree line.

Gaining elevation, we passed through stands of red spruce that replaced the white pines of the lower slopes and valleys. I mentioned to José that western white pines or limber pines grew right up to tree line in the Rockies. But not here in New England, he explained. They were less tolerant of higher elevations. He went on to explain that a fierce forest fire in the early part of the nineteenth century created a false tree line, as the trees had not yet come back due to the fact that the climate above 3,000 feet in New Hampshire was quite severe. Mount Washington, above 6,000 feet, had one of the most severe climates in North America, with winter winds clocking in at 250 miles per hour and temperatures dipping well below forty below zero (not counting the windchill factor).

Up here in a chilly northern forest of yellow birch (whose bark makes an excellent tea), Canada mayflowers coated the ground, and we stopped to listen to the notes of a warbler: twirl, twirl, twirl, zee, zee, zee. Its notes blended together with the distant notes of a black-throated green warbler somewhere up in the high canopy. We arrived at Falcon Spring to get an icy cold drink while chickadees chattered around us. José pointed to a 200- to 300-hundred-year-old yellow birch rising high into the forest canopy. We continued our climb past patches of hobblebush and mountain maples, which served as perches for Tennessee warblers and hermit thrushes, with their rich, ethereal notes piping through the woods. Ike had been so busy taking notes that he had to run to catch up with us. As he did so, we arrived at a dark-brown bog saddled between two lower summits beneath Monadnock. Here again we stopped to listen to a symphony of white-throated sparrows and hermit thrushes. I was reminded of my boyhood days along the coast of Maine, with its symphony of forest birds and foghorns at sea. All kinds of berries lay on the forest floor: bunchberries, mountain cranberries, and sandworts.

At last we arrived at the turtle shell of Monadnock and sprang up over the rocky summit to the very top at 3,166 feet in the cool and pleasant breezes (compared to the sweltering ninety-degree heat of Concord). We enjoyed sweeping views of eastern New Hampshire and the distant rolling hills of Vermont, draped in layers of cloud. We followed José down a different route to a seven-foot ledge overlooking five tall spruce trees, the exact location of Thoreau's campsite of early August 1860 where he feasted on cranberries and delighted in watching sunsets. Observing smoke-signal clouds from his camp, he wrote, "One evening, as I was watching these small clouds forming and dissolving about the summit of our mountain, the sun having just set, I cast my eyes toward the dim bluish outline of the Green Mountains in the clear red evening sky, and, to my delight, I detected exactly over the summit of Saddleback Mountain, some sixty miles distant, its own little cloud, shaped like a parasol and answering to that which capped our mountain."

We proceeded down a very steep and rocky slope into the rising humidity and heat of the valleys below, with occasional views into eastern New Hampshire lake country. It had become far too hazy to see in the distance another hill of Thoreau fame, Mount Wachusett, outside of Amherst, Massachusetts. None too soon, we six returned to Falcon Spring for a nice drink of water to refresh us for our hike back down to the valley below. Just remembering that icy drink in a steamy hot lecture hall the next day was enough to refresh me.

CHAPTER EIGHT

SOLACE OF DINOSAUR RIDGE

Quick iguanadons
Pitter pat along muddy
Beach with bright green eyes

Dinosaur Ridge has become an essential and necessary ingredient in my life since our move to Denver from a small university town on the wild and open prairies of Wyoming. Where would I have the freedom to roam and think in the urban sprawl of Denver? Where could I botanize and examine fossils? How would I stand the heat and smog of an August afternoon that would be cool and clear up in Wyoming? Where could I quickly get away from people and sirens and honking automobile horns? Piled on top of these concerns were the pressures, after a few years, of my deanship in an inner-city college with uniquely gifted yet disadvantaged students and a pressurized and strained faculty struggling with ever-shrinking budgets.

Within weeks of our arrival from Laramie, I discovered the small town of Morrison nestled behind an uplifted hogback formation called Dakota Ridge or, more fondly, Dinosaur Ridge. This magical piece of wild land lay only twenty-five minutes from central Denver. I took my first stroll along the trail, following the ridge top well over 1,200 feet above Denver after a heavy September frost. The city, smothered in mist and cloud, completely disappeared. I breathed the ridge's fresh and bracing air above the city's layers of cloud. That first walk along the ridge I repeated over and over again from September to April for twelve years straight. Sometimes I would go solo and sometimes with my wife and family, but most often with my little dog Mini, that golden English cocker spaniel with drooping ears and alert brown eyes.

This weekly ramble had become as much a ritual for me as my weekly walks on the Laramie plains. Summertime changed the Wyoming ritual with hikes in the alluring Snowy Range and now in the Front Range of Colorado. The high prairies of southern Wyoming have something very much in common with Dinosaur Ridge; namely, the Laramide Orogeny. Sixty to 75 million years ago, something within the Earth's core forced prehistoric swamplands (washed by the sea) upward. *If* four billion years could be transposed into one human life, the Laramide Orogeny raised the Rockies from sea level to almost three miles above sea level during the human equivalent time of two weeks.

The high, bald prairie of southern Wyoming rests at 7,200 feet, a thousand feet higher than the crests of Dinosaur Ridge. Inner forces of our planet are still pushing this land upward perhaps an eighth inch every century—not quite as fast as the growth rate of the Himalayas halfway around the globe. But the Laramie plains are essentially as flat as a seabed, while Dinosaur Ridge is a high, skinny ridge with downsloping Morrison Formation of gray beach rock on its east side and bright red Dakota Formation sandstone on its west side. The extreme north side is transected by Interstate 70. Why the name Dinosaur Ridge? Dinosaurs galore! Buried within the Dakota sandstones are the bones of stegosaurs, brontosaurs, and iguanodons, discovered by Arthur Lakes in 1877. Eventually, ten quarries yielded many fossils for rival museums in Philadelphia and New Haven. Today, Dinosaur Ridge is designated a national natural landmark. There are guided and self-guided tours along the base of both sides.

I love to visit one spot on the west side of Dinosaur Ridge that exposes the imprint of a brontosaurus made millions of years ago on an ancient muddy shoreline. The beast's immense weight sunk him deep into the mud. His tracks probably filled in with algal ooze, helping to preserve the footprints in hardened mud-rock. Lower down the ridge are fossilized rib and skull bones of camarasaurs, carried by streams and deposited in deeper mud that has been hardened to sandstone and exposed by erosion to present-day viewers.

On the east side of Dinosaur Ridge lies a strangely rippled rock (formerly beach) that has been hardened to gray sandstone and tilted at a ludicrous angle of forty-five degrees. Within this beach are giant three-toed tracks of a vegetarian dinosaur known as the iguanodon. Alongside his prints are three-toed prehistoric bird prints of an ostrichlike dinosaur. Early-morning shadows fill the tracks, clearly revealing their deep imprint. Because the beach is no longer sand but rock, and because the beach lies at an extreme angle, it is difficult to imagine a sea-level beach with heavy, humid air and swampy vegetation.

On one occasion, I took a quick walk along the east side of Dinosaur Ridge at sunset before boarding a jet the next morning bound for Charleston, South Carolina, to celebrate my brother's sixty-fifth birthday. Within hours of my arrival, I walked the Edisto Swamp Trail not far from the Georgia line with my brother and his children and their families. The geographic juxtaposition hit home. Here in the Edisto Swamp I breathed heavy, vaporous air, while hours earlier I breathed the bracing air of the high desert. At Edisto, I marveled at the delicate perfection of form and color of swamp orchids, the lush array of ferns and vine-covered southern pines, and the profusion of palmettos. On Dinosaur Ridge hours earlier, wind blew through the needles of pinyons and junipers. Deep in Edisto, I smelled mud and phosphates and thick vegetation. Up on Dinosaur, I smelled dust and rock and the scent of sage. Edisto provided a secure home for dinosaurlike alligators and other reptiles like the cottonmouth water moccasin. Edisto became for me prehistoric, Precambrian Colorado, whose oozing muds would eventually harden and be uplifted to a multilayered Dinosaur Ridge.

Interstate 70 cuts through Dinosaur Ridge and exposes all the layers of hardened pre–Laramide Orogeny sand and mud. As dinosaurlike trucks and RVs revved their engines up I-70, Mini and I walked through a hundred million years of time. We stared up at the cut-through formations ranging in color from gray to black to red to brown and yellow. Even though the heavy traffic of I-70 roared like a troop of dinosaurs, we managed to journey backwards through time.

I let myself dream of what things looked like 300 million years ago during the early Pennsylvanian Period, with its carboniferous jungles. I imagined looking westward to see an ancient mountain range 240 million years older than the present-day Rockies. This mountain range, like any other, had streams gushing off its slopes, depositing reddish quartz sand, silt grains, and clay. I tried to imagine these reddish deposits hardening into the red sandstone of the Fountain Formation and the Red Rocks Amphitheater of Beatles fame. But the only beetles I envisioned were black, creeping things on the muddy ooze of shorelines. What must it have been like 140 million years ago during the Jurassic Period? I imagined not seeing I-70 anymore and hearing the howl of meat-eating dinosaurs thumping through swamps and wetlands in an insufferably dank and humid atmosphere. What happened to Colorado? The only hint of its future existence lay in the gray and green and maroon clay-stone that would become the Morrison Formation.

I imagined escaping from wretched beasts to arrive at the late Cretaceous Period about 75 million years ago. Those frightening beasts hadn't yet left the scene, but now a great inland sea lapped the shore with tidal ripples in the mud covered by seaweed. The air remained heavy with no mountain breezes—just a flat swamp with bright, green-eyed iguanodons pitter-pattering along the mud in search of lush, fernlike cycads. Gigantic feathered beasts flapped their awkward wings above my head and cackled like mythological harpies. The tan, dark gray, and black shales oozed with mud and slime. I see that Mini has stepped into a mud puddle, and once again I hear the roar of I-70.

What I like most about Dinosaur Ridge is the relative peace and calm on top of its rocky spine. Up there grow yuccas, cacti, Gambel oak, pinyon pine, Utah juniper, sagebrush, mountain mahogany, kinnikinnick, golden banner, harebells, and scores of other wildflowers. Sailing overhead are ravens, hawks, golden eagles, and swallows. Nearby are buzzing hummingbirds. Mini, a ground-level cocker spaniel, simply loves it up here on the ridge between September and April, when there are no snakes to worry about. She loves to peer over the edge of cliffs and stare into space. All I have to say is "go see!" and she runs to the edge and takes it all in. She stops and listens to chickadees going chick-a-dee-dee-dee. She eyeballs each pine squirrel scampering up a twisted tree trunk. Even when she squats to urinate, she's all eyes for what's going on around her. Yes, she's a worthy successor to the dinosaurs of old.

At a certain narrow point on the trail's crest, I often stop and feel the texture of a rock, rippled and uplifted from that inland sea of millions of years ago. Algal materials covered earlier ripples and preserved their form when beaches became buried under layers of other deposits that hardened to rock. Tidal ripples are amazing to behold millions of years later—more amazing, in a sense, than the sarcophagus of the Emperor Charlemagne, or the Rosetta Stone. Why? Sixty million years! Imagine finding a 60-million-year-old plant in your backyard. How can one fathom the meaning of a wilderness of time found in 60 million years? A sand ripple is as common on the receded sea delta of the Colorado River down in Mexico as it was on the Great Inland Sea of ancient interior Colorado. But 60 million years separate the two ripples. Ripples we can understand, but the time between may be impossible. Or is it? We do have that special gift of Kantian intuition and Thoreauvian imagination. Dreams can cut through time like lightning through clouds to illuminate an otherwise darkened land. A stegosaur's roar and thumping step can still be heard in the spirit's core. The numbers sixty, 60 million, and 60 billion do not defy the human spirit. We can even imagine various species of dinosaurs having green flesh with orange spots.

I remember driving up I-70 one extremely windy day to an early January conference site on Lookout Mountain above Denver. Flames raced up the northeast slope of Dinosaur Ridge. Pinyon trees blazed with sparks that hopped up the ridge in a spectacle of beauty and terror. The blackened vegetation below the flames stood phantomlike in marked contrast to the whiteness of snow. Within days of my conference, Mini and I walked along that ridge top to inspect the damage. Mini sniffed the air and ground full-time once we arrived at darkened soil and blackened pine branches. Even snow had become dark with black and gray ashes, making for fertile soil next spring. Not too much damage here.

One mild February weekend we had a surprise visit from our son. My wife Maura and I packed a lunch for the three of us, with treats for Mini, to take advantage of the warm, pre-spring sunshine up on Dinosaur Ridge. Buds laced the branches of bare scrub oaks, and the most delicate and tiny flowers of sandworts graced the ground at our feet like miniature dots of snow. Arriving at a high sandstone upthrust, we stopped for lunch. The foothills of the Rockies spread westward and upward, obscuring the high Front Range. We could clearly see that our ridge protruded skyward as an uneroded shell fragment of an outer layer of sandstone and shale that once covered the Rocky Mountains. We finished our lunch atop the layers of time by recollecting our own family layers of time when Rich was a boy in Laramie with his two sisters, Michelle and Maureen. We all had a good reunion up there on the ridge. Rich now lived in Seattle and his sisters in New York and Fort Lauderdale—as spread apart as sediment from the Rockies that had traveled down prairie streams to the sea.

One crisp autumn day I hiked solo over the ridge when oak leaves had changed to bright scarlet. They rustled like prayer flags in the Himalayas. High in the foothills across the way, tongues of aspen blazed with a golden fire. Gray clouds swooped upslope like volcanic clouds millions of years ago when tectonic plates collided within the Laramide Orogeny. During our civilized state, we humans have experienced very little volcanism. Vesuvius, Etna, Krakatoa, and Mount Saint Helens were tiny firecrackers compared to the eruptions of the Yellowstone Caldera 600,000 years ago, when our primitive continent lay blackened for months on end. How frightening it must have been to see ranges of volcanoes puffing and exploding red-hot lava.

Snow sprinkled down from the upsloping clouds and gathered in windy wisps along my trail. A yellow-jacket bee buzzed for cover among the last of the autumnal flowers still barely in bloom. It snowed yet harder in chilling winds, and the sky darkened. It felt good to be up here; I could have easily been hundreds of miles away. It grew even colder, and some leaves blew off the scrub oaks. My hands and feet grew numb, and it was time to make my descent to the cares of the city below. Chickadees along the trail chirped to bid me farewell.

Yes, I'm glad I discovered a place called Dinosaur Ridge. Up there, my urban-encased being is truly energized and revitalized. It is a place of magic—magical realism. It is a place that allows the spirit to roam free through time and space.

CHAPTER NINE

A CLOSE CALL ON MOUNT PRINCETON

I had wanted to climb Mount Princeton (14,197 feet) ever since my late friend Mark Reames suggested ascending this mountain several years ago. I grew up in Princeton, New Jersey, where my father served as a reference librarian at Princeton University for nearly twenty years after he had managed Parnassus Bookshop in Princeton during and slightly after World War II. Mark was a Yale man who had climbed the higher Mount Yale but never Mount Princeton; he wanted to broaden his Ivy League experience. Most important of all, after our climb, we would soak in Mount Princeton's hot springs just outside Buena Vista, Colorado.

Even after Mark's unexpected and tragic death from a fall in the mountains above Boulder, I still wanted to climb this mountain and arranged to do so with my son, Rich, and friends Jonny Boucher, Gordon and Walt Fader, and Michael Mackey. We attempted to climb Mount Princeton (without Jonny Boucher, who was detained by his mother's illness) in early August 1997.

We woke up at our campsite in chilly air with a steady, light rain and, wearing our ponchos, ate our breakfast bars and oranges. We soon trekked up a steep and winding gravel road under slowly brightening clouds. Reaching the tundra around noon, we ate our lunches in the shelter of a small cave that protected us from increasing winds and pelting snow mixed with sleet. Michael Mackey opened a can of sardines for his lunch and succeeded in fuming up the cave as though it were some fisherman's cache on the seacoast in the west of Ireland. We quickly exited the cave and proceeded along the trail with barely fifty feet of visibility. Our ponchos flared out in the wind like giant bat wings. Should we continue? We decided to go around the next bend to see how it looked. Other descending climbers, all covered with a thick layer of snow, warned us not to continue, as hurricane-force winds were raging on the upper ridge that led to the pyramid-shaped summit. However, we slugged along the trail for another quarter mile with freezing hands and feet and ponchos almost ripping off our backs. After Walt Fader and I almost slipped off the trail, I finally said we must turn around. All reluctantly agreed. This was my first unsuccessful attempt on a Colorado fourteener. We had made it to an elevation of slightly more than 13,000 feet in this fierce storm with decreasing visibility. What would we have ever seen from the summit had we managed to get there? Even the visibility back in Denver a day later proved to be incredibly limited, with freak thunderstorms and hailstorms dumping ice pellets so deep that snowplows were brought out to remove as much as two feet of hail from city streets in early August.

One year later, almost to the day, my English friend Jonny Boucher arrived in Colorado to climb Mount Princeton shortly after he finished a fifty-mile trek in the Pyrenees. This summer's ascent would mark the fortieth anniversary of our climb with Gordon Fader of Mount Katahdin in northern Maine. We booked a campsite at Mount Princeton's base for four nights straight in case we had to wait for bad weather to abate. That evening, Jonny, myself, and a young, French-speaking college student, Herve Picherit, watched rain clouds gather and lightning fork the sky. We felt certain that we would not be able to climb the next day. But several hours before we turned in for the night, the stars came out, along with a thin, Arabic sliver of moon. The narrow valleys filled with gossamer threads of cloud that spread in slow motion to our very own campground, where a crackling log fire snapped with as many sparks as there were stars in the sky. Jonny chatted a good bit about his great Spanish hike along the pilgrims' trail. But now he was very anxious to climb his second American mountain and the second highest—some 5,000 feet lower than icy Kilimanjaro.

The next day dawned clear, with the strong scent of pines freshened by the rain of the day before. As we ate our breakfast bars, we watched pert Canada jays hop from branch to branch, begging for food. We packed our gear and carefully drove our four-wheel-drive vehicle as far up as tree line just in case we needed to make a rapid retreat. Unthinkingly, I drove atop a higher knoll, not wanting to get blocked in by other cars. I was glad to have that open space slightly above the narrow, winding road, as several other cars followed us. Shouldering our packs, we sprung out onto the tundra, which was covered with thick patches of yellow alpine avens, and deftly handled the first rocky ridge at about 11,800 feet. Another series of ridges loomed above with alpine harebells, chiming bells, and alpine gentians (cousin to arctic gentians), all bright blue, lacing the damp ground. Mist rose up from the rain-soaked valleys only to be burnt off by the bright alpine sun. Here we were on the upper approaches to Mount Princeton, a far cry from walking the Princeton University campus in front of Nassau Hall on the way to Firestone Library! Jagged slopes of other collegiate peaks, including Yale and Harvard, rose in the distance. Marmots' squeaks echoed from alpine rills to alpine walls.

We stopped for water and caught our breath. The air of almost 13,000 feet started to get to us, along with the challenge of yards and yards of upsloping loose, wobbly rocks. I paused to rest my legs and enjoy the rare beauty of yellow, orange, and green lichens that abundantly coated the boulders all around us. Alpine thistles swayed on their stalks in between a jumble of rocks. This was a far cry from sitting in the warmth and comfort of my father's 1940s bookshop in Princeton and listening to young poets the likes of W.S. Merwin, Galway Kinnell, and William Meredith.

We climbed yet another false summit to peer out onto alpine heights looming above, and the lower couloir, where we had been forced to turn around in fierce winds last summer. Squawking ravens circled the skies. At our feet were two inches of fresh August snow from last night's storm. We paused to eat oranges while sitting on black rocks (Princeton University's two colors) and to rest our wobbly knees. We knew we must summit the final peak no later than noon for fear of afternoon thunderstorms christening us with rain and lightning bolts. Black storm clouds gathered to the west, but thankfully they remained distant. We three huffed and puffed to reach the pointy summit at 14, 167 feet. We sat under a rock cairn to catch our breath and chat with several other climbers. Silently we celebrated our achievement high above the misty veils of clouds, pierced here and there by imposing peaks. Pikas screeched from the ledges below us, seeming to beckon us to descend.

Our descent route led us over steep, downsloping, wobbly rocks gurgling with deep underground streams that reminded both Jonny and me of our descent of Mount Katahdin forty years ago—an underground concert of trickles, drips, and gurgles. Even though Jonny spent the past forty years in banking and I in academe, we had a lot in common, particularly our love of mountains and our love of Asia. The descent was so steep at times that my toes painfully crammed into the front of my boots. As we passed "fish" cave, where we ate lunch a year ago, we reflected that it had been a wise choice then not to try and reach the summit, as it took us nearly two hours of rapid descent to arrive here *without* blowing snow and howling winds.

We left the trail to cross over to our car, which was perched on its lonesome knoll. I immediately put the car in four-wheel drive, low gear, and tried to ease it down the hill to the winding road below. But neither low gear nor the brakes held nearly as tightly as I had hoped. As we gained speed, I had to make a quick decision to turn sharply right at the road and probably bang into other cars, or to turn sharply left and hang tight above a steep drop-off, which would have been disastrous should we have hopped right across the road. I managed to bring the car left onto the road and follow the two ruts faithfully until I stopped the car to breathe a sigh of relief. Jonny simply said, "In Fleck we trust." All we could think of was a good hot soak in the steaming springs down at the foot of towering Mount Princeton's lower chalky white cliffs and a nice cup of hot tea at our campfire that night.

CHAPTER TEN

RAMBLES ALONG THE MOSQUITO RANGE

Views from the Mosquito Range are phenomenal. Look across the valley to the west and you see Mount Elbert and Mount Massive, usually blanketed in snow, rising above 14,400 feet. To the southwest loom Princeton, Antero, and La Plata, and northwesterly rises Mount of the Holy Cross. Yet, when I first saw the Mosquito Range in the distance from the top of storm-tossed Mount Ida, those peaks, too, looked amazingly tall and snow-blanketed. I knew I must explore them someday, not realizing that it would be more than thirty years after my ranger days. Usually the middle three peaks of the Mosquito Range—Lincoln, Bross, and Democrat—can be climbed in one day. Way above Kite Lake, there is one enticing spur ridge between Democrat and Lincoln called Cameron Peak; if climbed separately, it counts as a fourteener. The northernmost peak is Quandary Peak, just outside of Breckenridge, and the southernmost is Mount Sherman, which some mountaineers who have recently climbed Crestone Needle consider a joke. It is nothing more than a high green hump. But so, too, is Mount Bross, only Bross is a higher green hump that bears amazing resemblance to Green Mountain, a prairie ridge that rises to the east of Dinosaur Ridge. All of these mountains were heavily mined for gold and silver, traces of which can be still found in slag heaps beneath ant-hole mines that fairly well prickle the side of Mount Democrat. On the Leadville side of the Mosquitos, the mountains are still being gouged by gigantic molybdenum mines at Climax. Mount Lincoln pitches high above the valleys below, with its dark pyramid of rocks forming the highest bit of peak.

Permit me to begin with Mount Sherman. Yes, it's far less of a challenge than Crestone Needle, but it does provide a workout, surely more so than Mount Evans from Summit Lake. In fact, it proved to be a challenge for the women with whom I climbed one day—the first time ever that all of my alpine companions were female, including my wife and two doctors, one from Maine (Allison) and the other from Texas (Crystal). The doctor from Augusta, Maine, developed a breathing problem at about 13,000 feet. She slowed down to a crawl, and we all stopped for her to rest. After Allison drank some hot tea, she perked up and continued her slow, methodical trek. Crystal served as her coach with words of encouragement, especially after Allison said she couldn't make it. Within thirty minutes, Maura and I stood on the final approach to the summit and waved back down to Allison and Crystal to show them they had but a little way to go. I turned back to rejoin the two doctors and walked slowly with Allison, allowing Crystal to summit with Maura. When Allison saw nothing but sky above a stony ridge, she knew she could make it, and that she did. We all applauded her as she wearily walked up to the cairn and breathed a sigh of relief at 14,036 feet. Refreshed with cheddar cheese, crackers, and tea, we all stood up to enjoy the distant view of the Sawatch Range, beginning with Tabeguache and rolling northward to the Mount of the Holy Cross. Allison regained that sparkle in her eye as she stared out into endless alpine terrain and sky.

The wind picked up and a band of thick, gray clouds formed and spread from the west, making us all a bit anxious. We donned sweaters and parkas as the temperature dropped by several degrees. It was time to make our descent. We easily hopped down the stony trail to a saddle overlooking an abandoned mine. The sky grew grayer. Tufts of sunflowers bobbed in the wind. Pikas squeaked as if to warn us to quicken our pace. Just as we approached the old gold mine far above the winding gravel road back to Fairplay, it began to spit sleet and rain. We put on our baseball caps and trotted down the last bit of slick ridge to arrive at the road and our car in a torrential downpour. Mount Sherman proved to be challenge enough.

My daughter Maureen from Florida had not yet climbed a 14,000-foot peak. My son Rich had not yet ascended Mount Democrat. The three of us and my son's dog, Boo Radley, departed for Alma early last August while my wife babysat our three grandchildren. We turned onto the Kite Lake road and quickly gained elevation up to 12,900 feet, switching back and forth past abandoned gold mines and splashing through streams. All the while, Boo sniffed the air and constantly yawned noisily in anticipation of our arrival. Anticipatory yawns, I call them. Not a cloud in the sky! Kite Lake glistened in the rising sun. The air was chilly.

My Floridian daughter bundled up in a heavy sweater and hooded parka, while Rich and I shouldered our packs. We stopped along the trail to admire bright yellow sunflowers and light blue harebells, but not Boo. He dashed up and down the slope at least six times. Ravens circled above, letting out raucous squawks. Pikas and marmots squeaked and whistled as we climbed up to another abandoned mining shack surrounded with small stalks of alpine bistort. Up here, the temperature was even chillier. We put on our gloves and proceeded up toward the saddle between Cameron and Democrat. Halfway there, we stopped for a bit of trail mix and admired the view of kite-shaped Kite Lake far below. We couldn't help but notice numerous mining scars above, some silver in appearance, some golden. Boo dashed ahead to wait for us, along with dozens of other dogs, at the saddle. We three slogged along, stopping now and then to catch our breath. But not Boo. He stood patiently, cocking his head, up at the saddle. When we finally arrived, Rich rewarded Boo with a treat, and we rewarded ourselves with small chocolate bars as we stood and gazed at the mountainous terrain to the west, at huge Mount Democrat rising to the south, and at Cameron Peak looming to the north. A far cry from sawgrass and palmettos!

Somehow I had remembered gentle switchbacks going up Democrat a few years earlier with our neighbors Mike and Crystal. But that was an illusion. Instead, the trail proved to be quite steep, with loose gravel, rolling stones, and tricky switchbacks. Boo had no problems. We three trudged along, carrying on a conversation that was constantly interrupted by huffs and puffs. This side of the mountain was devoid of almost any vegetation. The wind increased as the temperature decreased. At last we saw people resting against the sky a few hundred feet higher. They stood, of course, on a false summit, and Boo soon joined them.

"What kind of dog is he?" they asked.

"Part Border collie and part lab. See his webbed feet?" Rich said. Meanwhile, the beast dashed off to the left of the trail to sniff rocks where other dogs had paid liquid homage. Once Maureen arrived at this ridge line, we pointed up at the last bit of summit atop a hundred-foot pile of rocky slabs. Dutifully, we hoofed onward, trying to keep up with Boo, until we stood at the very summit. There we high-fived with Maureen to celebrate her first fourteener at 14,148 feet, or slightly more than two and a half miles above her home in southern Florida. It was a great occasion for our family as we gazed around at a full sweep of mountainous space.

On another occasion, Cameron Peak, across the way from Democrat, was our goal as Maura and I hopped out of the car at Kite Lake with our neighbors Mike and Crystal. We had planned this climb as a farewell get-together with Mike and Crystal, who were moving to Oregon a few days later. We had to make the climb on July 1, a tad early for completely summer conditions. From Kite Lake we looked up at deep, menacing banks of snow lining the trail. Nonetheless, we proceeded up to the abandoned mine without any difficulty. Alpine avens and snow buttercups sprouted out of the edge of melting snow. The sky was azure blue and the temperature chilly. We all put on our gloves and continued huffing along until our trail led us to the base of a very deep snowfield. Above, it looked clear pretty much up to the saddle. Mike and I broke a trail for the women by wading up to our knees and sometimes up to our hips. Maura seemed frightened. To alleviate her fears, I walked above Maura while Mike walked below her, each of us holding one of her arms. We walked slowly for fifty yards and caught her if she slipped until we got to open land once again. We returned to Crystal, who was twenty-five years younger than Maura, and got her through the long patch of snow quite quickly. Maura, in the meantime, had become hesitant about continuing upslope, but we assured her that she had gotten through the worst of it. Fortunately, the trail remained open all the way to the saddle, where we rested and ate snacks. The view back to sparkling Kite Lake proved rewarding. A few more climbers trudged through the broken snow below, waving thanks to us for clearing the way.

We easily avoided smaller patches of snow on the way up to Cameron's summit, but our legs were a bit tired after the snowy episode below. We hardly noticed frail chiming bells bobbing in a gentle breeze along the switchbacks. Red-tailed hawks swooped the ridge lines far above. We talked of our friends' move to Oregon and our trip the following year to Ireland, Maura's homeland. Mike asked if there were any hills to climb back there. "Not like this," I said. But I explained there's nothing prettier than the green and lush Mountains of Mourne in County Down. They are carpeted with pink fields of heather and occasional patches of lush, sweet blueberries. On the flanks of Slieve Gullion, one of the Mountains of Mourne, there is a dense plantation of new forests resembling what ancient Ireland must have looked like when Celtic tribesmen hunted stag deer and black bears. Except now, as I explained to our neighbors, the forests consist of Alaskan Sitka spruce and Norway pines. Those rolling green Mountains of Mourne sweep right down to the sea.

A sudden gust of icy wind brought us all right back to Colorado. Trail dust blew in swirls into our eyes and nostrils. We at last reached the upper spiny ridge, and it was an easy hop up to the snowless summit at 14,238 feet. We found a hollow that was out of the wind and stretched out on the ground to rest our weary bones. Then we sat up and ate some cheese and salami sandwiches and drank hot tea. Restored, Mike and I got up to look across at the high pyramid of Mount Lincoln rising to the north, but as time was fleeting, and they had to finish packing for Oregon, we slowly made our descent to the saddle and through the snowfield back to Kite Lake when nothing was left but memories.

And what of Lincoln and Bross? I had earlier climbed both of them solo via the same route up the saddle and to the crest of Cameron, but on this occasion I pushed on to Mount Lincoln by way of a charming piece of tundra tucked below the north face of Cameron, with Mount Lincoln rising a mile away. I had discovered a marvelous bit of deserty alpine tundra with a whole colony of succulent little *Lewisia*, which had occasional pink blooms bursting forth from fleshy rosettes of greenish-yellow leaves growing out of stony soil. I had never before seen such a profusion of vegetation at this altitude just shy of 14,000 feet. I felt like staying here the rest of the day just to enjoy this small piece of Hawaii so high in the sky.

But, I forged ahead along a trail connecting Cameron to Lincoln at the very edge of the western ridge line. There was a drop-off of several thousand feet down into glacial cirques laced with snow and ice fields. Within half an hour, I found myself climbing the last bit of a rocky summit, which involved a few foot- and handholds, until I stood atop Mount Lincoln at 14,286 feet, the eighth highest peak in Colorado. I peered straight down into an endless abyss separating Lincoln from Quandary Peak, with its long incline and final hump of a summit.

I remember having climbed Quandary on the latest date ever for a fourteener—mid-September—with Mark Reames. On the way up, under the clearest of skies, we admired browning tundra peppered with alpine gentians and dwarf rosy paintbrushes. It was a splendid day. Mark and I talked of our experiences in Japan and that, although we didn't know each other at that time, we lived across the Nigawa River from one another. Sometimes the Reames family noticed an American family carrying groceries across the river and wondered who they might be. We met eight years later as colleagues at Teikyo Loretto Heights University, a Colorado branch of a Japanese university. Mark and I worked on developing a "Colorado Experience" curriculum for first-year Japanese students. Colorado would be the focus not only in writing classes but also in history, photography, and biology classes. All faculty would get together with the students on Saturday field trips up Mount Evans, where students would keep journals describing the krummholz zone of bristlecone pines. They would collect and press plant specimens, take black-and-white landscape photographs, and read Enos Mills and other Front Range writers to gain historical perspectives on earlier-day Colorado. One student wrote a paper for my English class saying, "Trees on Mount Evans are shaped by wind. *No.* They *are* the wind!"

"Did you ever do anything like that with Japanese students in Japan?" asked Mark.

"No, but surely I did so with my family."

"Did you climb any mountains in Japan besides Fuji San?" he asked.

"Yes, quite a few coastal hills, including Miya Jima Yama, Kabutoyama—an extinct volcano near our home—and Rokko Mountain. I remember climbing up Rokko Mountain on the trail of the fire Buddhas. I couldn't get over how thick the cobwebs were between trees. They actually crackled as you passed through them."

Mark laughed.

"I remember walking very gingerly when I spotted a deadly poisonous *mamushi*, a viper snake that is brownish-black in color. He wound his way uphill parallel to me until I arrived at the first fire Buddha overlook. Then it slid into some undergrowth beneath blazing-scarlet maple trees (*momiji-wa*). Just seeing a statue of the Buddha with flames coming out of the top of his head purified me of my fear."

"Well, there are no *mamushi* up here," Mark said gleefully as he pointed across at Mount Lincoln.

We proceeded up to the base of the final steeper summit when I suddenly experienced a leg cramp. Mark had a worried look on his face, hoping I would not give up on the final assault. I stomped my foot on the ground several times and the cramp thankfully disappeared. White upcroppings of shiny granite shone brightly in the September sun. They looked like marble glistening in the Italian Dolomites. We at last stood atop Quandary Peak at 14,265 feet and opened our lunch sacks. Mark surprised me with a fresh tomato picked from his garden that morning. We counted thirty other 14,000-foot peaks from up here, including all those in the Mosquito, Front, and Sawatch ranges.

But here I stood in brisk air atop Mount Lincoln, gazing across at Mount Bross. What the heck, I thought. I'll go for Bross as well. The wind increased to such a velocity that I had to hold on to my sunglasses or have them ripped off my face. Once I descended to the ridge line that joined Cameron with Lincoln, the wind, thankfully, decreased from furious to steady. I followed a trail eastward toward Bross but lost even more elevation into a grassy meadow at the base of Mount Bross, which rose to 14,172 feet—104 feet lower than knobby Mount Lincoln. The meadow lay a thousand or so feet below the highest knoll of Mount Bross. Replenishing myself with trail mix and Gatorade, I easily bounded up the gentle incline, stopping several times to look across at Lincoln and Cameron. Sunflowers cropped up all around me, as did clumps of alpine bistort and king and queen's crown, lending dots of color that resembled a Georges Seurat painting. Hawks and ravens circled above, letting out high-pitched whistles or raucous squawks, respectively. A few mud tunnels lay exposed from melted snow—the workings of pocket gophers.

I scanned the afternoon sky to see thunderheads building up over the Sawatch Mountains to the west. Time to finish my ascent and plan a route back to Kite Lake. Should I go all the way back to Cameron and descend a rocky trail to the saddle between Cameron and Democrat? Or should I explore the possibility of a quicker descent route directly from Bross itself? Several teenage boys stood at the rock cairn marking the summit, and as I approached, I waved to them. At the windy summit, I shared some trail mix with them and asked their advice on a descent route to Kite Lake. They gleefully advised me not to go all the way back to Cameron Peak, but to simply follow the trail southeastward along the flanks of Bross and then make a rapid descent to the valley below. They mentioned that the trail would be steep and that I would sometimes have to sit and slide down, controlling my speed with my feet. Bad advice for a man in his mid-fifties (at the time), as I had to contend with weaker knees than teenagers. Worse yet, I followed their advice.

The trail along the flank proved easy enough, as it descended at a very gradual rate. Once I arrived at the south side of Bross with a bird's-eye view down to sparkling Kite Lake, I had to make a sharp descent to a lower spiny ridge that jutted out over the valley. In order to do this, I sat down and slid on the seat of my pants for thirty minutes until I reached the plateau below. But the kids didn't say which way to go from here—right or left? The trail forked and went both ways. I chose the right side facing Cameron Peak. I descended on wobbly knees until the pitch became nearly vertical. I sat down again and inched my way very cautiously, thinking to myself that this could not be the trail. If only I had my usual trail companions with me! I happened to spot the tiniest of human figures far below. This ant-sized figure seemed to be signaling. But signaling what? I took off my sunglasses and squinted at this figure. What the heck was he or she trying to say? Then it dawned on me that the person was violently waving his or her arms upward toward me. I got it! Slowly I inched my way backward, daring not to turn around. When I say inched, I mean inched. It took me more than an hour to slowly scuttle back up to that plateau overlooking Kite Lake. Perhaps guardian angels can appear in the tiniest of forms. Once up there, I tearfully noticed that clearly the trail to the left was more heavily used. Although I had to sit down and slide on the seat of my pants, I did so with a big grin on my face, because now I could see a series of switchbacks a hundred feet below me. Arriving at the first switchback, I gave thanks and enjoyed every foot of the way down. I stopped frequently to admire crinkly monument plants, spongy moss, springy elk sedge, and an ever-enlarging Kite Lake. It was amazing to see dwarf spruce and willows at my feet; amazing to breathe rain-soaked air to the west; amazing to hear rumbles of thunder miles away; and amazing to hear distant human voices from the trail far below me. Western song sparrows chirped. Very fat marmots waddled across the rocky terrain before me.

It was simply great to arrive at more level tundra that was soft underfoot. I smiled at everyone I passed along the shoreline of Kite Lake—no longer a gleaming little eye in the tundra seen from far above. Solo climbs are indeed spirit builders, but they can be more risky than they are worth. I had no trouble that night falling into a deep sleep!

CHAPTER ELEVEN

MULTIPLE ASCENTS OF MOUNT EVANS AND PIKES PEAK

My parents and I wound our way up a twisting mountain road in my 1939 Chevrolet. I had taken the day off as a park ranger-naturalist in Rocky Mountain National Park to show my visiting parents some rugged alpine terrain outside the national park and higher than Trail Ridge Road—in fact, the highest paved auto road in North America. This was the road up Mount Evans to 14,200 feet. The last sixty vertical feet to the summit had to be walked. Just the other day we all had felt the distant tremors of the great 1959 earthquake in Yellowstone. We certainly hoped we would not experience a light aftershock up here on this narrow road, with no bumper rails separating our moving tires from a 2,000-foot drop-off. My mother's eyes showed fear, if not panic, as I steered the car around each sharp turn on our way to Summit Lake. I tried to calm her by pointing out the window at fields of alpine sunflowers that were almost as yellow as the sun itself.

"Keep both hands on the wheel," she said, while she secretly prayed for a level stretch of land.

My father, on the other hand, was all eyes for the vast panorama of prairie that spread far below, forming a great arc of horizon. He mumbled to himself, "God, what country!"—an important statement considering he was agnostic.

"What are those animals?" he asked suddenly as we wound around a curve.

"Rocky Mountain goats," I said with a gleam in my eye.

My mother immediately seemed to calm down when she rolled the window down to stare into their brown eyes after I stopped the car. She was simply amazed at their gracefulness and beauty as they danced through a snowfield as white as their fur. She started to laugh when she recalled repeating what one smart-aleck graduate student told her back in Princeton—that nature had marvelously accommodated mountain goats' anatomy to mountains by giving them two shorter legs on one side so they could more easily walk around steep slopes. She had naively repeated this bit of information once in Parnassus Bookshop when there was a lull in the conversation among professors and poets. The poet John Berryman had roared with laughter, saying, "What happens if they change their direction?" We drove a bit farther with smiles on our faces to the Summit Lake parking area and got out of the car to take a wee ramble.

Out on the solid, flower-strewn tundra, which was so antithetical to smoggy, industrialized New Jersey, my parents began to relax and take it all in. We had brought along some sandwiches and a thermos of coffee, and when we arrived at some flat gray rocks, I suggested we sit down for a tundra picnic. This was their first trip west of Harrisburg, Pennsylvania. They, of course, underwent a kind of "shock of geography," but the longer they remained above 12,800 feet, the more accustomed to the land they became—especially with the rather awesome glacial cirque of Mount Evans forming a backdrop. There was nothing back east to begin to compare with the vastness of the Rocky Mountain West. They never had the opportunity of seeing Mount Katahdin in northern Maine, although my father had done some rambles along the misty Appalachian Trail in the White Mountains of New Hampshire. Rugged though the White Mountains are, they just don't quite measure up to the vastness of a titanic Mount Evans.

After lunch, and after delighting in a close inspection of miniature alpine-forget-me-nots, I suggested we drive up to the summit of Mount Evans. Although a bit of fear returned to my mother's eyes, she and dad did seem resolved to continue up the highest paved road in North America. Since they had explored 12,200-foot Trail Ridge Road in Rocky Mountain National Park just the other day, I had selected this piece of terrain so that they could experience—for the first time ever—life above 14,000 feet.

Once they stood at the benchmark of 14,264 feet and stared out into planetary space, I knew they were hooked on the American West, where they would retire a few years later. They would open up a mail-order antiquarian bookshop in Laramie, the spirit of old Parnassus Bookshop in Princeton back in the 1940s, and would even have numerous walk-in customers. You can bet that they stocked western Americana!

Some thirty years after this car trip, I had the occasion to lead groups of Japanese students from Teikyo Loretto Heights University in Denver along the tundra beneath the summit of Mount Evans. We traveled up there in rickety old school buses whose engines overheated with steam pouring out. While they cooled down, my group of students, doing their "Colorado Experience," squatted down to make pen-and-ink sketches of delicate alpine vegetation. Such sketches would line the borders of their English compositions written about the alpine heights of Colorado. Other groups took photographs or botanized, depending on which instructor they were with. As it became late afternoon, the air temperature dropped considerably. I suggested that my students and teaching assistant finish taking notes for their future compositions and finish their sketching. In fact, we were the last group up on the mountain as we strolled back to our school bus. The driver nervously informed us rather solemnly that our bus had broken down. He had worked on it all afternoon, to no avail. He was going to wait for the tow truck.

Now it was quite chilly, with the sun being a mere red ball on the western horizon. What were we to do? Fortunately, my teaching assistant, Tony Tadasa, spoke fluent Japanese. He explained to the coeds that they must forget their false pride and hitchhike back down to Echo Lake Lodge. He finally succeeded in getting some of them to stick out their thumb and hitch a ride, but there were very few tourists left up there in darkening skies. In fact, nine of us remained. What would we do? They really needed warmer jackets to begin hoofing downslope from around 13,800 feet to Echo Lake Lodge. Nonetheless, we began our cold hike down.

Something told my Teikyo colleague, Reuben Ellis, that all was not well up on the mountain. Even though he was speeding past Idaho Springs, he decided to turn around and drive back up in his four-wheel-drive Wagoneer. We had all managed to descend by a half mile or so when Reuben suddenly appeared. I have never seen such wide smiles on students' faces. All nine of us crowded in—some sitting in the cargo section, others jammed into tiny spaces—and we happily journeyed back to the city of Denver, all reiterating our experience.

After my Teikyo years came a series of climbs with different people, starting at Summit Lake at 12,800 feet. Once it was with my wife, along with Michael and Ellen Mackey; another time was with my son and his dog Boo; another was with Scott Martens, my Iowa niece's husband; and yet another was with Gordon and Jean Fader, my niece Missy, and Missy's husband John. On that occasion, I served as a guide for an otherwise entirely sea-level crew. Gordon, of course had climbed with me in Maine and Arizona, but all the others had never climbed a mountain of any sort before. And yet, they all did incredibly well, especially in crossing a snowfield at a thirty-degree angle. Jean, the artist, brought along her sketch pad for the summit and had a photograph taken of her sketching at 14,264 feet—all smiles. But the going down proved quite tiring to all of them. Their knees became wobbly, and their stomachs growled with hunger pains. Although Jean limped a bit on the way to the parking lot at Summit Lake, she would never have given up such an experience on this cloudless day in July. Gordon was pleased as punch to have made three climbs with me—Katahdin, Wilson, and

Evans. My niece and her husband returned to Charleston, South Carolina, with a fourteener under their belts.

The most memorable climb of Evans was the one with my wife and our dog Mini. We didn't simply climb directly up from Summit Lake, but went all the way around the glacial cirque and approached the summit from the west side for an all-day hike. Backpacks shouldered, we hoofed around to the west shoreline of the lake and its marsh marigolds and proceeded up a series of rocky humps well above 13,000 feet. Each ledge we crossed lay embossed with beds of alpine flowers, including bright blue dwarf columbines growing out of rocky crevices.

We paused to drink water, eat trail mix, and throw Mini her treat. Just over the next ledge we gained a broad view of a very green plateau. Four mountain goats grazed in the distance, and Mini cautiously kept her distance. This piece of terrain reminded me so much of Medicine Bow Peak west of Laramie. My mind drifted back to the early 1970s, when my son was just five years old.

West of Laramie and east of Saratoga, an alpine haven humps upward over 12,000 feet, laced with named and unnamed lakes that are surrounded by creaking spruce and Indian paintbrush, and where hawks are always circling high above. No matter what the season, those glittering snowfields look like some vast Moby Dick rising up from the rolling prairie floor. Their lure is hard to resist. Up there in the Snowies, the alpine seasons fuse with summer that bursts into fall, which is snatched by winter gripping the approaching spring.

One morning late in July, as I played ball in the backyard with my little boy Rich, we couldn't help but glance westward toward Medicine Bow Peak.

"How would you like to climb Medicine Bow today, Rich?"

"Is it hard to climb?"

"It's a joy to climb."

We packed our lunch and soon found ourselves on the winding trail above Lewis Lake. Putting on our sweaters in the biting chill of the wind, we passed patches of pink "watermelon" snow gleaming under an intense sun. I remember years back tasting some of that red-algae-ridden snow and suffering nausea and aching bones for three long days. Rich didn't dare even whiff a handful of pink snow, although I told him it smelled just like a watermelon cut open.

When we reached the saddle beneath Medicine Bow Peak and Sugar Loaf, my son asked, "Do you think I can make it?" He looked a bit tired, but I encouraged him to climb up the switchbacked trail through evergreen brush and scrawny stands of willow to a spot overlooking Lewis Lake. Here we had our sandwiches and hard-boiled eggs coated with salt and pepper. We ate fresh oranges for dessert, and did that trickling juice ever taste good to our parched mouths! Afternoon thunderheads slowly built up as we got up and started our gradual trek upward. Little swallows flicked past our heads. Rich wanted to take frequent rests, but, after an hour of steady progress, we came to the edge of a steep snowfield, where we had to inch our way straight up, cutting steps as we went. At one very steep pitch, I carried my boy a few hundred feet. His weariness completely disappeared from his face as he crawled across the last hump of snow to the summit. It was good to see the joy in his eyes as he looked far to the north at Elk Mountain, with a rumbling thundercloud hovering just above it.

Mini barked several times at a fluttering raven just above her head. I asked Maura if she didn't think this spot on Mount Evans looked like the Snowy Range up in Wyoming. She agreed, and we reminisced about our annual Labor Day climb of Medicine Bow Peak with Rich, Michelle, and Maureen.

"The next time Michelle and her husband Rob come out for a visit, we'll have to take them up Mount Evans," I said.

"Do you think we can make it all the way up this side of Evans? We've been at it for quite awhile," Maura said.

"Let's give it a try."

We took another rest while looking across at a lightning-bolt-shaped snowfield that dropped off the west face of Mount Evans. The three of us proceeded over some jagged ledges and were afforded a grand view of Mount Bierstadt, rising a thousand feet above us with a steep abyss in between. Other climbers coming down from Evans told us that we had less than a half-mile to go. We followed the rock cairns up a forty-five-degree pitch above Abyss Lake. I could tell that Maura was beginning to feel uncomfortable, especially after we had to push Mini's pumping hind legs in midair under a ledge that she couldn't quite manage on her own. We sat down for some Irish tea poured from our thermos and waved at other climbers, who told us the west arm summit was just above us.

Feeling a bit better, Maura got up. We followed more sets of cairns and arrived at the west arm in a matter of minutes. Mini stood at the very precipice and stared straight down at Summit Lake. Instead of hiking the crest line over to Mount Evans' slightly higher summit, we bounced down the tundra on the back side of the mountain, crossed the highway as it wound around to the front side, and soon strolled across a gentle ridge overlooking Summit Lake. We all slept well that night, although once or twice poor Mini woke up whimpering.

Rich, his then-fiance Jess, and I chose to spend our Fourth of July climbing Pikes Peak from the west side, beginning at Crags Campground. At first we had difficulty finding the trail; in fact, we never found it. We simply ascended in a southeasterly direction through a dense evergreen forest until, at long last, we emerged onto the tundra from a rather steep, rocky ridge. We heard a strange buzzing sound in the distance which proved to be racing cars! We had totally spaced out the annual Fourth of July race up Pikes Peak. We dashed across the gravel road only to see Bobby Unser's car whiz past us at some incredible speed. Despite the noise, we took time to enjoy a groundcover of spring beauties, parry primroses, alpine forget-me-nots, and alpine sunflowers against an azure sky.

Obviously, we could not follow the gravel road up to the very summit. Instead, we traversed the plateau so far above Colorado Springs and scrambled up the last several hundred feet of ledges and boulders coated with crusty lichens. At times, our view down sheer faces of cliff proved frightening, especially with irregular gusts of wind. While we were dressed in hooded parkas up there above 13,800 feet, we couldn't help but notice the steam-heat of the flat plains 9,000 feet below. No wonder this mountain generates its own weather. It is the only fourteener that rises directly up from the prairies. As a result, cold, downsloping air collides with the hot, sultry prairie air of July. Once this happens, storm clouds develop seemingly out of nowhere. I have never witnessed such violent hailstorms as I have on the Palmer Divide far below Pikes Peak. The entire ground can be covered with a thick layer of summer hail.

We stopped for a rest just 100 feet below the summit. As expected, thunderheads built up in the distant western horizon. Jess looked a bit nervous, but I explained that going down the mountain would be considerably quicker. When we reached the summit, thankfully the car race had finished. We walked over to the restaurant and snack bar—the only fourteener in Colorado with such a facility—and I ordered three plates of jalapeño-smothered nachos and soft drinks. Rich and Jess looked at me rather doubtfully. Was I in my right mind? But we sat down, and in minutes our plates were empty.

"A strange but great choice, Dad," Rich said.

Our conversation at a 14,110-foot dining table proved to be a bit whacky. We all giggled at almost anything and seemed to have difficulty choosing words. But then thunder rumbled in the distance. We left the building quickly and started our long descent back to our car. It proved to be fairly easy descending to the plateau and following the tundra ridge line to the point where we could see, far below, the crags of our trailhead. But which ravine should we descend? Rich discovered a trail, to our great joy, but the trail soon petered out at tree line. Rather than climbing back up, we cast our lot with the valley below and bushwhacked our way down. This proved to be quite tiring, and Jess looked worried.

To pass the time during our steady descent, I remarked that at least this going down wasn't as dangerous as the occasion I had on Slieve Gullion in Northern Ireland. They both asked me why. I explained that once I stood atop Slieve Gullion and looked all around at the green universe of Ireland; the IRA raided a British garrison in the valley directly below where my car was parked. Instead of following the winding trail back down through heather and pine, I took a shortcut, all the while listening to tracer bullets and high-velocity rifle fire. Two British choppers flew directly below me and headed for the Fork Hill Garrison. By the time they fired a few rounds, the raid was over and silence had returned. Nonetheless, I kept descending at a rapid rate to get back to my car just above Fork Hill.

I dropped into a small vale to arrive in a thick, oozing peat bog with clumps of ferns and rich green moss. Part of the bog had been cut to drain. Eventually, bog farmers would haul out tons of thick brown peat for turf fires in the cottages below. Black choughs flew overhead, with their orange bills highlighted in the afternoon sun. I had to be very careful taking this shortcut crossing the bog by stepping on vegetated clumps; otherwise I would sink up to my hips in watery moss. When I got across the bog, I climbed over some steep, treacherous rocks covered with thick moss. Suddenly slipping, I grabbed an exposed root as I would have done in the Rockies, but the root pulled right out of the moss, and I fell backward into a boggy hole.

Mountaineering in Ireland requires you to take unusual precautions. Although the rifle fire had stopped completely, I wanted to get back to the car and get out of there just in case it flared up again. I finally climbed out of the bog, crossed a field laced with luscious blueberries, and descended a steep hill to my car.

Jess asked me what I did then. In reply, I told her that I avoided the town of Fork Hill completely by following an unimproved gravel road and "jumped" the border back into the Republic of Ireland. It wasn't long until I pulled into the driveway of Maura's old home at Tullyraghan, where I told my story of the day and was at once served a tall glass of black Guinness with a creamy head and some tasty wheaten bread.

Here on the west flank of Pikes Peak it was beginning to get dark, but we could see the rocky crags no more than a mile away. We were all quite weary as we brushed through pine branches and bramble. We could have surely enjoyed a glass of Guinness at that point. When we hopped into our car, the last traces of daylight lingered in the northwestern skies. We relived that climb all the way back to Denver.

CHAPTER TWELVE

MOUNTAINS OVER THE DESERT

"Late in August the lure of the mountains becomes irresistible. Seared by the everlasting sunfire, I want to see running water again, embrace a pine tree, cut my initials in the bark of an aspen, get bit by a mosquito, see a mountain bluebird, find a big blue columbine, get lost in the firs, hike above timberline, sunbathe on snow and eat some ice, climb the rocks and stand in the wind at the top of the world on the peak of Tukuhnikivats."

—Edward Abbey, *Desert Solitaire*

I remember first going to Arches National Monument with my father after we both had read Abbey's *Desert Solitaire* a few weeks after it was first published in 1968. We got up at three in the morning and left Laramie for the town of Dinosaur, Colorado. As tempting as it was to stop and explore Dinosaur National Monument, we continued driving south on a rolling, deserty road to Grand Junction and westward to Moab. The arches formations looked exactly as Abbey had described them—a fantastic array of orange sandstone fins suspended in midair and gigantic chess pieces balancing precariously high above scrub junipers and pinyon pines. Soon my father and I proceeded along the trail to the Delicate Arch under cobalt-blue skies with tiny ripples of cloud. As the trail gained altitude up over slickrock, we both had the distinct impression that this was Mars; the bright orange-red soil lent credence to our impression. But yucca, prickly pear cactus, desert poppies, and scraggly sagebrush convinced us otherwise, unless we tramped over a martian landscape now rich in oxygen.

We stopped to drink some water and eat peanut-butter sandwiches and chips. A desert wren flicked past us, and a pinyon jay, as blue as the sky, perched itself on a pine branch above our heads. We climbed to the top of a high mound of sandstone overlooking miles of desert. At one point, we edged along a narrow cliff until we rounded the far side of it to be afforded a fine view of Delicate Arch perched, as delicately as a pinyon jay, above a plateau of wrinkled orange sandstone.

Approaching the arch, we could see ever so clearly the mountains of the desert—the La Sal Range—rising, snowcapped, in the distance. The Spanish explorer Escalante named the mountains "La Sal," thinking they must be covered with salt, not snow. How could it be otherwise in such a hot desert? The name has stuck ever since. Their name may, after all, be quite apt. Ten million years ago, the La Sals were formed by inner volcanic uplifting of much older collapsed salt deposits to form giant, unbroken blisters called laccoliths, through which no volcanic materials etruded. These laccoliths gradually gained their prominent shape through millions of years of erosion and glaciation to become spectacular mountains above the desert.

We ended our journey at a point where Delicate Arch framed those mountains. White snow and desert heat! Stark and empty foreground and wispy white mountains in the background. Yes, my father and I could see why Edward Abbey needed to climb up and out of the desert to a pinnacle of rock in celestial space. They are an amazing biogeographic island in the desert on which grow a unique species of flower—the rayless daisy (*Erigeron mancus*)—found nowhere else on earth. It would be some thirty-five years later that I, too, would experience this unique alpine island.

The La Sals are second to the Uintas in height in the state of Utah. They are a relatively short range, being only fifteen miles long and six miles wide, just east of Moab. There are more than ten peaks above 12,000 feet, with Mount Peale being the tallest at 12,721 feet—among the highest in Utah. The other peaks have an array of colorful names: Tukuhnikivats (Where the Sun Lingers in Ute), Talking Mountain, Tomasaki, Mellenthin (pronounced melon-teen), and, on the east side, Mount Waas. They are usually blanketed with snow from November to April and the highest of the La Sals sparkle with snow well into July. They, like the Uintas, have lush forests of lodgepole pines, aspen, spruce, and fir. It is quite a pleasure to the eye to see them from the Colorado River north of Moab near Fisher Towers, but even more pleasant to be up in them.

Michael Mackey and I sat in our folding camp chairs with steaming mugs of tea late in the day in a high alpine meadow above Geyser Pass. We were looking across the way to Mount Mellenthin, which was catching the dying rays of sun. Although the marsh mosquitoes of late June buzzed our ears, nothing could disturb us as we watched a dark shadow creep across the western flank of Mellenthin—we could see the shadow slowly move across upper scree of that mountain, now covering a partially lit rock with total darkness. As the sun sank below the western horizon of a golden desert far below, Mellenthin began to turn from dark gray to rosy pink. It was pure alpine theater, and no buzzing mosquitoes or fluttering millers could break the spell. Slivers of upper snowfields appeared to have become huge slices of watermelon; white-throated sparrows added musical accompaniment to the show. And then, as our own meadow darkened in the chill of an early summer evening in the La Sals, the entire western sky glimmered with an alpine glow.

Getting up here to set up camp certainly wasn't as pleasantly cool as this evening. After witnessing miles on end of bushless dirt mounds and dry washes along Interstate 70, we turned off at the Cisco, Utah, exit and headed toward the Colorado River and the distant La Sal Mountains, which loomed like phantoms above the desert. The closer we got to the canyon of the Colorado, the more dense the desert vegetation became, including sagebrush, rabbitbrush, and thickening groves of sweet-smelling tamarisk. It was such a relief to finally drive along the shorelines of the churning and thrashing Colorado River. We followed the river for a dozen miles or so until we entered Castle Valley, with the bright red Fisher Towers and a series of buttes called the Professor Rocks looking like giant human figures cowled in graduation robes. At last, the La Sal Loop Road!

Ever upward, we climbed past tamarisk and juniper bushes and pinyon pines, which then yielded to extensive groves of scrub-oak trees rustling in the dry desert winds. Ravens circled the skies above while riding the thermal layers of air. And then came lush groves of tall, graceful aspen trees. Somewhere near an elevation of 7,000 feet, we turned onto a steep gravel road leading ever upward toward Geyser Pass at 9,500 feet. Beyond the aspen groves, we entered dense forests of Douglas fir, Englemann spruce, and subapline fir. My, how cool it had become as we stood outside the car at Geyser Pass, scanning the meadows for the ruts of a four-wheel-drive road. We discovered several sets of ruts but chose a pair that led northward toward the flanks of Haystack Mountain, looming above the pass. Finding an ideal spot for our campsite at 10, 000 feet, we pulled over and unloaded our gear.

We talked of Edward Abbey later that evening as we sat around a nice crackling fire. He certainly obtained relief up here from that hot desert sun in Arches National Monument, as it was called in those days. In fact, it felt like Ed was with us that night, although we had forgotten to bring an after-dinner bottle of German wine to share with him. He drove his jeep up to about this altitude forty years earlier, just below the talus-laden slopes of steep Mount Tukuhnikivats. In the chilly air, after supper, he laid out his bedroll, which was still warm from the desert below, and soon dreamed of his ascent the next day. Abbey, at the time, was thirty-five years younger than I was, and my stamina for several thousand feet of loose talus slope had dwindled considerably. Not that a much younger Michael and I would not experience loose and sliding rocks the next day! We both believed that Abbey was a remarkable person and remarkable writer. But clearly, he was a much better essayist than he was novelist, and clearly, we reflected that night, *Desert Solitaire* remains a classic to this day. I told Michael of another friend of mine from Japan who was also an Abbey aficionado. He had planned to translate *Desert Solitaire* into Japanese. But, as he said, the title alone proved to be as difficult a challenge as the loose scree of Tukuhnikivats. How do you get into Japanese the double meaning of the words "desert solitaire?" That is, to play a philosophical game of solitaire, not with cards, but with the desert, and at the same time, to live and think in solitude (not loneliness) in the desert. By the time Professor Minoru Fujita thought he might be ready to start translating, he was beaten to the punch, but the Japanese edition that did get published had a totally unsatisfactory translation of the title *Desert Solitaire*.

On that hot August day, Edward Abbey needed the yin of the snowy La Sal Mountains to balance the yang of sandstone fins shimmering in heat waves. After he woke up at dawn at his mountain campsite, he ate a quick breakfast and bounded up the loose talus, sometimes slipping, certainly sweating and grunting, and eventually standing on the high summit of Tukuhnikivats, looking down on the shimmering desert heat of endless miles of red sandstone and alkaline flats and seemingly Mars itself. What a fine haiku of contrast—snow, chilly air, alpine granite, squeaking pikas, and rosy finches fluttering above tree line so far above searing, dry heat, hazy dust, cactus, Spanish bayonet, yucca, pinyon jays, and parched, sandy soil.

I slept outside that night near the glowing embers of our campfire. The insects had calmed down, and the stars seemed to swirl across the black sky like Vincent van Gogh's "Starry Night." I listened to the symphony of white-crowned sparrows in the surrounding woods and heard the footfall of mule deer grazing in the meadow where Michael and I had watched the alpine show on Mount Mellenthin. A meteor flashed across the sky with a green streak. I dozed off until four in the morning, when mosquitoes began to buzz through the air, along with clumsy millers. It was chilly—mighty chilly. I pulled the cord of the sleeping bag tight to mummify myself, and I dozed off again for another hour or so until I heard a fantastic symphony of song sparrows, white-crowned sparrows, and Swainson's thrushes: *Mc vie a doo, mc vie a doo, A-tee-tee-tee-tee, A myrtle, a turtle, a wurtle, Mc vie a doo*. Again a clumsy miller brushed past my ear. I had to get up. It was dawn. Indeed, there is more day to dawn, as Thoreau exclaims. I walked out to the meadow to witness a different alpine show. Mount Mellinthin caught the eastern rays of an unrisen sun (from my standpoint) and began to glow with a bright tangerine color. Mule deer pranced below me, and an eagle sailed above. I walked back to the camp and lit a burner to make some coffee. Michael began to stir inside his tent. In minutes, we both stood around a stick fire made from the still-glowing embers and drank coffee between bites of breakfast bars. Time to pack for our climb of nearby Haystack Mountain.

We followed a trail through a spruce and fir forest until we emerged into a bright alpine meadow blanketed with chiming bells, alpine avens, red-berried elder, and prickly squaw currant bushes. After building a small cairn of rocks atop a flat stone to mark our return trail, we aimed our way toward Haystack Mountain, which rose to our left just above tree line. We walked across hardened pocket-gopher mud grooves that earlier served as tunnels through deep snow. What busy creatures they are. Crossing several trickling and icy rivulets fingering their way through marshy ground, we approached a high grove of spruce trees just below a 300- or 400-foot-high slope of loose talus framing the blue sky. At this elevation, in the Colorado mountains, one would find numerous twisted and weathered limber pines, but not so here. There is no such thing in the isolated La Sals. Arriving at the base of talus, we sat down for a rest, munched on some trail mix, and took swigs of orange Gatorade. We leaned over to admire delicate clusters of purple alpine forget-me-nots, deep pink parry's primroses, and white moss campion, and looked all around us for the unique rayless daisy—but saw nary a one. It remained pleasantly cool so high above Moab. We both wondered if Abbey had not sought the relief of the La Sals more often than he wrote about. I know I sure as hell would have. But then, my ranger days were served high in Rocky Mountain National Park, not Arches, so perhaps I would need the La Sals more than Abbey did. I remember the time when I traveled through the Utah and Arizona deserts headed toward the Grand Canyon while still a ranger in Colorado. I so missed my Colorado Rockies when I was out there in the greasewood flats of the desert. And then the road began to climb up out of the desert into the fresh, lush forests of the Kaibab Plateau. It was so nice to be back among the aspen and spruce!

Like Abbey, we, too, began our cautious ascent of loose and wobbly talus slabs formed by millions of years of freeze and thaw and thaw and freeze. They seemed to be like a very slow-moving glacier of rocks. But they can move fast, alright. I crept up the slope carefully and slowly, more slowly than Michael, who climbed ten or fifteen yards higher than I did. Not as much lichen on these wobbly rocks as their equivalents in the Colorado Rockies! I looked up and there stood Michael, all smiles, on a false summit of Haystack Mountain. A minute or two later, after several zig-zags, I joined Michael and stood and stared into the vast space of the lower desert. Michael pointed toward the higher cairns marking the summit of Haystack Mountain, and we proceeded along the flat rocks and onto a gently rising snowfield leading toward the summit. We gingerly crossed several smaller snowfields and stood at the summit to look southward at a not-so-high Mellinthin and the much higher Tukuhnikivats, Talking Mountain, and Mount Peale, the highest of the La Sals, rising not quite to 13,000 feet. We checked our wind-torn map to find the names of peaks to the north: Tomasaki, Manns, and La Sal. Snowcapped peaks and shimmering desert make for a La Sal experience.

Abbey, feeling the need to return to desert reality, selected a Tukuhnikivats snowfield, tested it by throwing a flat rock on it to see how fast it would go, and soon followed the rock down a flank of Tukuhnikivats somewhat too fast. Fortunately, he came to a roaring halt just before some sharp, jagged rocks. All too soon he turned on the ignition of his vehicle to drive back down to a desert ignited with furnace heat. What is desert reality? Abbey explains just why he chose the desert: "I am here not only to evade for a while the clamor and filth and confusion of the cultural apparatus but also to confront, immediately and directly, if it's possible, the bare bones of existence, the elemental and fundamental, the bedrock which sustains us."

We weren't quite ready to make our descent because we didn't have a descending snowfield to lower depths as an option. We ate more trail mix and continued to enjoy the view of mountains above the desert. From here, we could clearly discern how narrow they were. From Geyser Pass, they immediately sloped downward both east and west, with just a narrow ridge between. They were only six miles wide—truly an island in the desert.

We began our descent back across the snowfields to the very edge of the false summit overlooking a steep slope of talus. Michael started first and I followed, being careful not to be exactly above him in case I caused a rock or two to slide down. At one point, halfway down, a rock slid a few inches, causing me to sit down rather abruptly. From this position I stared at tiny dots of shining cars creeping along the La Sal Loop Road far below. A lone jet raced across the sky, creating a vapor trail. Not many jet routes cross the La Sals—perhaps this jet was on a Minneapolis–Las Vegas flight. I cautiously arose and proceeded with many zigzags through the scree down to the meadow below, where Michael sat eating an energy bar. We high-fived it after I made it down. Again I looked for the elusive rayless daisy, with no luck. I wished that the one and only guidebook of the La Sals had, at the very least, a picture of this flower—that might have helped, perhaps.

After we passed through the small stand of Englemann spruce, we looked down at several meadows, not knowing which meadow might be the correct one for our return trail. I suggested sticking to a higher contour line and following it for a half-mile around to a large meadow. But once we arrived there, it didn't look right. Three or four meadows lay far below. Which one should we go to? For a moment I was reminded of my early ranger experience, when I ascended Mount Ida from Lake Julian in Rocky Mountain National Park, only to look down on three lakes, not just one; I wondered which one was Julian, where my friends awaited me. Of course, I chose the wrong lake on my return journey. I paid for my mistake with eighteen hours of tramping through trailless valleys to the Colorado River and civilization.

Here in Utah, we rapidly descended to a lower meadow, but it wasn't the right one! Michael suggested going through an aspen grove and hopefully coming out at the right spot. What had we to lose? We came out at the wrong meadow. In the worse-case scenario, we could freelance it down to Geyser Pass right under Mellinthin and hike back up the four-wheel-drive road to our campsite. Instead, we proceeded southwesterly through another aspen grove to see, at last, our cairn above a meadow trail. All too soon we arrived back at the campsite, broke camp, and drove down to Geyser Pass and to the lower La Sal Loop Road. Like Edward Abbey, we descended to the heat of Moab for a refreshing lunch. Out on the streets of Moab again, stunned by the heat, we looked up at the snow-streaked La Sal Mountains, wondering if we had ever been there. Were they mere phantoms of our minds? The desert can do things to you like that.

A FINALE

SACRED BLACK HILLS
(Paha Sapa Wakan)

Part I — Up Laramie Peak

We passed Fort Laramie in the night, and on the seventh morning out we found ourselves in the Black Hills, with Laramie Peak at our elbow . . . looming vast and solitary—a deep, dark, rich indigo blue in hue, so portentously did the old colossus frown under his beetling brows of storm clouds.

—Mark Twain, *Roughing It*

In Mark Twain's day and earlier, Wyoming's Laramie Range was considered part of the Black Hills. About the time Mark Twain went west to the Nevada Territory on his overland stagecoach journey, a Black Hills treaty known as the Treaty of Fort Laramie was signed in 1868 by Lakota tribal leaders and federal agents, stating specifically that the Black Hills were to remain Indian territory and that whites could mine gold and carry it out via prescribed wagon roads. But under no circumstances would non-Indian settlement be allowed. For the Lakota people, the Black Hills were and are the center of the universe, where the good road and the road of despair cross. They are a place of visions. Black Elk, holy man of the Oglala clan of the Lakota tribe, believed that these hills held special significance. Not only were they essential to the practice of the sacred rites of his tribe, they also gathered in thunderclouds, or thunder beings, which provided him and others with a special vision to help his people remain whole.

In order to acquaint myself with these sacred mountains, how could I dare ignore Wyoming's old Black Hills? No better place to start than Laramie Peak, considered by some to have the most classic pyramidal shape of any mountain in the west. Pink puffs of clouds fleeced the eastern horizon of Laramie, Wyoming, as I drew the curtains aside and awaited my climbing partner, Dick Barbour. After a second cup of coffee, I hopped in his jeep, and Dick and I forged northward toward 10,274-foot Laramie Peak in the balmy air of dawn. A haze hugged the Snowy Range to the west, putting to mind Henry Thoreau's poem, "Wool of the Sun, Ethereal Gauze," which is woven of "Nature's richest stuffs." The pink clouds gradually whitened with the rising sun, and mountain bluebirds fluttered along the telephone wires.

Distant, dark Laramie Peak remained remote until we turned onto a prairie gravel road north of Rock River and drove directly toward the mountain. The entire Laramie Range spread southward from Laramie Peak, looking quite bald with only a few vegetated spots here and there. I remember camping up there once, south of Laramie Peak, with my family in a sheltered aspen grove, to be awakened several times by hooting owls under starry skies. At dawn's early light, the Snowy Range to the west lit up with a pinkish-red hue, which gradually changed to brilliant gold. On other occasions we would go up into these hills to gather ripe chokecherries to make a nice wild pancake syrup inspired by our Shoshone friends.

Now, a covey of sage hens strutted in front of our jeep and proceeded up a prairie knoll. They seemed so unaware of our presence, vehicle and all, that we could have thrown pebbles at them and they would not have flinched. Several pronghorn antelope bobbed up and down as they danced across the prairie, catching sunlight on their white rumps. As we turned onto the Garret Road considerably northeast of Rock River, Wyoming, we immediately became aware of a change in landscape. Rolling prairie gave way to upcroppings of granite dotted with jack pines, somewhat reminiscent of South Dakota. More and more knife-rock hills appeared here and there as we bounced along the dusty road.

To me, the country before us appeared as what I imagined Australia to look like, but instead of wallabies and kangaroos, antelope grazed along dried-up streambeds. Dick and I became so entranced by this "down-under" landscape that we missed our turn and had to backtrack to pick up the Laramie Peak road. We drove up a steep hill overlooking a ranch house just like the one in the movie *The Big Country* (without Charles Brickford) and a rustic red barn. Forest lands lay a few miles directly to our east. After opening and closing several barbed-wire fence gates, we proceeded toward Bear Creek and suddenly plunged down into the creek, worrying if we would ever get across. But the jeep bounced up over a steep eastern bank and bounded into a dense, trembling aspen grove, with Laramie and Eagle Peaks looming high above. The aspen leaves fluttered like some sort of spirit beings.

Large, sweet, vanilla-smelling ponderosa pines rose into the sky all around us. We crossed several soft meadows of tall grass, sunflowers, and fireweed. A mile later, we arrived at Friend Park, a grassy meadow surrounded with lodgepole pines, ponderosa pines, and aspen trees. The air was sweet and warm as we put on our hiking gear to proceed up the five-mile trail to the summit of Laramie Peak.

Pine squirrels scurried along the branches above our heads as we scuddled up the trail. A young mule deer pranced through the ferny woods in a vale just below us. We began to feel like we belonged to the land especially after feasting on juicy wild raspberries and tiny little grouseberries that peppered the vines at trailside. High pinkish cliffs loomed above us—we could even hear the wind rustling through pines that clung to those cliffs several hundred feet above. With a few swigs of icy canteen water, we pushed on up the winding trail. Canada jays and Clark's nutcrackers squawked in the dense forests as the pink cliffs gradually sank below us.

The closer we came to the summit, the steeper the trail became, sometimes at a forty-five-degree angle. There were switchbacks every fifty feet. A few cascading streams tumbled out of boulder-strewn cliffs, softened with clusters of bright blue chiming bells and Colorado columbines. Those boulders got larger and larger as we gained elevation. Where was the summit? It had to be the next pinnacle—but no. After a half-hour of huffing and puffing, that next pinnacle stood far below us. Many moons later, I would make use of this experience in my novel *Clearing of the Mist*, in which Fort Laramie cavalry units pursued Indians up Laramie Peak. One of the soldiers was an Irish immigrant who saw a parallel between starving Irish during the potato famine and the tribal people, causing him to switch sides.

Dick and I finally caught a glimpse of a relay antenna high atop the bald peak above us. We stopped to rest and drink more water. The trail became steeper and more winding. But on we plodded up the dusty trail through thinning trees. With a final spurt of energy, we climbed over the last hump and out onto the narrow ridge that overlooked a quarter of the state of Wyoming.

Hazy valleys below glistened in the sun. Distant Elk Mountain to the west darkened in a patch of cloud. The Snowy Range to the southwest and Casper Mountain to the northwest spread before us. We couldn't help but notice dark, pine-strewn ridges fingering their way eastward all the way to the rising Black Hills of South Dakota. Surely these old territorial Black Hills were truly connected to those of South Dakota. The exhilarating air we breathed helped us forget the tiresome agony of the trail below. We nibbled on fresh peaches and sandwiches, which restored our energy as we chatted with a few other fellow climbers who had reached the summit—one fellow for his fifth pilgrimage. He pointed out a hermit's shack in a hazy valley far below—an ideal place for solitude and contemplation in noisy modern times.

Distant thunder rumbled and growled as we signed the summit register. We hopped down the trail, doing our own mountain spirits' dance. Halfway down, thunder boomed and rumbled from cliff to cliff, and the peak itself appeared as Mark Twain described it, with a beetling brow. Sheets of hail pelted us as we trotted through fields of Indian paintbrush. Without gloves, my hands became cold and numb. All too soon we arrived at the jeep and headed back toward Laramie, nestled beneath giant thunderheads all cast aglow by the setting sun.

Part II — Thunder Beings of Harney Peak

> From West to East a summer offering is made
> where thunder beings, thunder beings, thunder beings,
> rising white above the black of lower clouds,
> catch a rosy glint from the golden West.
> Up they rise, ever higher, up to the Spirit,
> the Great Sprit, the unifier, the unifier
> sending fire down in bolts, jagged bolts,
> scorching the wet green land pelted white where
> grasses sway and bend in rushes of wind
> and cottonwoods clidder in torrents of rain
> infusing matter with spirit across the plains
> as rumbling thunder recedes to dark of East,
> and above the land stars glisten in the sky.

Some thirty years later, all winter long I anticipated our climb of sacred Harney Peak (7,242 feet), the highest point in South Dakota. Fortunately, during the winter I taught two classes that read *Black Elk Speaks* and other books relating to Lakota culture. *Black Elk Speaks* is a bi-autobiography of Black Elk, holy man of the Oglala Sioux, as told to John G. Neihardt in 1931. As Black Elk explains to Neihardt, "It is the story of all life that is holy and is good to tell, and of us two-leggeds sharing in it with the four-leggeds and the wings of the air and all green things; for these are the children of one mother and their father is one Spirit."

At the very young age of nine, Black Elk, during sickness, was given a vision of harmony in which he was taken to the "center of the universe," which was Harney Peak in the heart of the Black Hills. There he was shown the "Flaming Rainbow Tipi," where six grandfathers showed him the way to harmonious living within a sacred hoop of the nation. Each of the six old men gave Black Elk a power to achieve this harmony, whether it was from the sacred North or East, South or West, or from the Sky above or the Earth below. It was very important that he listen with his heart and spirit to the old men, as bad times were coming to the Lakota people in which their spirit would be broken by they who were many, or the white men. Young Black Elk was given the power to make live through thunder beings, the power to heal through the sacred herb, the power to make peace through the sacred pipe, the power to make whole through the flowering red stick, the power to transcend space through astral projection, and finally, the power to transcend time through maintaining the core of his youth even in old age. When the grandfathers left and the Flaming Rainbow Tipi disappeared, there stood Harney Peak. Black Elk and his people had a tough road to travel as they went through life from buffalo hunting to the battle with Custer, to Wounded Knee, and to reservation poverty, including the loss of their sacred Black Hills to gold miners and settlers. Not only had the Black Hills provided his people with food and water and tipi poles for shelter, they provided visions sought and visions given. Even though they became physically "owned" by gold miners and others, the Black Hills will always continue to nurture the Lakota spirit.

In late May, my wife Maura and I drove north by northeast to these "hills," with the intent of climbing Harney Peak. I don't think I'll ever see again thunder beings of clouds so impressively metamorphic as those that gathered in a northwest-to-southeast line following the contour of South Dakota's Black Hills. I watched them as Maura and I drove from Lusk to Newcastle, Wyoming, on our way to meet our hiking companion at the Rapid City airport. Those puffy white cumulus clouds shape-shifted from one type of being to another: an opened-beaked eagle, a lurching coyote, a rumbling buffalo, a sacred dancer with an arched back, an elderly man holding pointed hands above his ears. They all just hovered above the still, invisible Black Hills, but you knew that those mountains were there because of their sky companions hovering above.

Meanwhile, our companion, John Borusheski, had just left his business meeting in Sacramento. An oh-so New Yorker at the meeting asked him, "So where is it you're flying to after here?" John answered, "Rapid City." "Oh," said the New Yorker, "I'm sorry."

We entered the hills whose dense stands of ponderosa pines had been recently blackened with forest fires—some two years ago, some last year. Buffalo grass grew back strong and softened the black soil with its gentle new growth. I looked up at the clouds, which now had become just clouds that were layering the sky like ordinary clouds anywhere. Lush green meadows reminded Maura of her native Ireland. Windows lowered, we could catch the melodious notes of western meadowlarks, as rich as a thin sheet of hammer-tapped gold lining an altar of some Tibetan temple. These Black Hills began to tug at the psyche. They emanated some sort of invisible ray almost like the very visible fingers of pine-studded ridges connecting Laramie Peak and the old territorial Black Hills to these. Something more than cloud, geography, and mind came together here. We continued our drive through Custer, past the still-crude giant rock carving of Crazy Horse, through Hill City, past Mount Rushmore, and down to Rapid City and south to the airport. John's plane landed as we stood by a display case containing a Lakota headdress and other implements—the display case from the movie *Thunderheart*. John ambled along the walkway with other passengers—he was all smiles. We greeted one another and talked of Harney Peak. Maura pointed to it outside the airport. "Yes, I saw it out the plane window," he said.

We arose early on the next very gray morning and proceeded back up into the Black Hills and Sylvan Lake. We hoped it wouldn't rain on us all the way up Harney Peak. We could hardly see Sylvan Lake; we only saw just a bit of rocky shoreline. Mist hovered overhead, with the slightest droplets of fine rain sifting down from the faintly thundering sky. We shouldered our packs and talked of Black Elk. In 1931, the old Oglala holy man told poet John G. Neihardt, as he pointed toward Harney Peak, "There, when I was young, the spirits took me in my vision to the center of the earth and showed me all the good things in the sacred hoop of the world. I wish I could stand up there in the flesh before I die, for there is something I want to say to the Six Grandfathers."

John, Maura, and I talked of the Six Grandfathers representing east, south, west, north, sky, and sacred earth. Our feet touched the earth with each step we took up the gentle trail, scented with vanilla from the bark and sap of ponderosa pines. Although the sky remained heavy and overcast, distant notes of western song sparrows and white-crowned sparrows lent us some cheer. But the higher we rose through the woods, the brighter the sky became. The brightness of the sky was further accentuated on the ground by many sparkling, mica-coated rocks along the trail. We passed large, gray, overhanging boulders of granite and walked over to an open rocky ledge to the side the woods, which afforded us a grand view eastward of granitic badlands—a hobgoblin of rocks, some looking like shawled women, others like climbing turtles, and still others like perched owls. We noticed with joy that the sky had almost completely cleared, and a strong sun illuminated pine needles and rock as well as our inner spirits. Maura seemed delighted as she rambled along the trail with her walking stick.

John G. Neihardt helped arrange a trip to Harney Peak for Black Elk in 1931, as recorded in *Black Elk Speaks*. On the way up to the summit, the old man said to his son, Ben, "Something should happen to-day. If I have any power left, the thunder beings of the west should hear me when I send a voice, and there should be at least a little thunder and a little rain." Black Elk's climb had begun under intensely blue skies. It was dry and warm. Thunderclouds seemed unlikely.

We continued upward past clusters of turtle rocks. Gradually, ponderosa pines received new neighbors of aspen and Douglas fir. Buffalo grass was pleasant to the eye. The trail rounded a corner and began to *descend*. We worried that we might be on the wrong trail. It descended past Indian shawl rocks farther and farther down toward a soft green meadow. Along the way we paused to admire lush rock coatings of green moss—Irish green moss. But still the trail descended. We began to doubt that this was the right trail. What we needed, however, was patience. Soon we splashed through a stream and began to climb up through metamorphosed woods, now all lodgepole pines, so called for providing the Lakota people and others with tipi poles. While we hiked along in the warm sun, to the east and south it remained densely misted.

Black Elk and fellow climbers arrived atop a cloudless summit during a season of fierce drought—the memorable drought of the early 1930s and Dust Bowl days. When he was a young man in the late 1870s, Black Elk went on a vision quest (*hamblechya*) and perched himself on one of the high, rocky domes atop Harney Peak. He fasted and prayed for several days when a terrific thunderstorm approached him. Bolts of lightning forked the sky. Hailstones slanted down in a sick, gray-green light toward young Black Elk. He thought for a moment he would be slashed to ribbons. But amazingly, the hail stopped just a few feet short of where he sat praying. Rumbling thunder slowly subsided. He knew he had been given the power of the thunder beings. He would be a thunder-being person to serve his tribe during the encroachment of *wasichus* or "they who are many," who were coming from the east in search of gold and land and earthly power.

We proceeded higher through glistening lodgepole pines, with a few scattered higher-altitude spruce trees. Maura paused to point out a delightful view down the cliffs into a sunny wetland below. She told us to listen to the spring peepers. John and I stopped to listen to this peaceful woodland chorus. We all took swigs of canteen water, feeling as thirsty as buffalo on a dry prairie. As chipmunks scurried through the ground cover, we stopped once again, this time to listen to the distant piping of a Swainson's thrush from the forests below. And then we came upon it! Placed on a rock just below the final summit lay a beautiful Lakota prayer bundle, a cluster of flag cloths in six different colors: red for the rising sun of the east, yellow for the golden warmth of the south, black for the thunderheads of the west, white for the snowy north, and brilliant blue for the sky above, mated with chartreuse green for the sacred earth (*unci wakan*)—indeed, the Six Grandfathers. I sensed that the *wichasha wakan* (holy man) Black

Elk would be happy looking down on this prayer bundle, making the *Paha Sapa* complete, even if the U.S. government had failed to return these hills to the Lakota people to make amends for the broken Treaty of Fort Laramie.

We picked our way up the stone steps to the uppermost rocky summit of Harney Peak in the clear sunshine high above the veils of mist pushing up against the Black Hills from the east. On another rocky ridge just to the west—perhaps the one where young Black Elk sought his vision—we spotted a pure white Rocky Mountain goat with his black horns gleaming in the sun. The whole place emanated with energy. We felt like staying up there forever.

As we ate some trail mix and looked into the six directions, another hiker named Gary joined us at the summit. He had moved out to South Dakota from the crowds of the East. He had lived here in the Black Hills for ten years. John asked him what he thought of Mount Rushmore and the Crazy Horse Monument. He said, "I guess I'm old-fashioned. I like things the way they were a hundred years ago. To me, it's wrong to carve anything into these rocks. Let them be. They are, after all, held sacred by the native people."

I asked him what he liked about the Black Hills. "Oh, I guess I like their beauty, their eagles, the increasing number of mountain lions. I think there are around 300 of them now in the Black Hills. I like the whitetail deer and the mule deer. I don't know, these hills are a self-sustaining piece of terrain on this tired old planet."

"What do you think about the native people?"

"I think," he said, "they are coming back stronger. Have you ever been to Bear Butte or Devil's Tower? They've placed prayer bundles and prayer flags all around them. That's beginning to say something—that there's more than gold in them thar hills."

We all listened to him intently. Maura looked particularly pensive.

Old Black Elk dressed and painted himself in the presence of John G. Neihardt and Ben Black Elk. As recorded in *Black Elk Speaks*, he exclaimed, "Hey-a-a-hey! Hey-a-a hey! Hey-a-a-hey, Hey-a-a-hey! Grandfather, Great Spirit, once more behold me on earth and lean to hear my feeble voice.... All things belong to you—the two-leggeds, the four-leggeds, the wings of the air and all green things that live. You have set the powers of the four quarters to cross each other.... Therefore I am sending you a voice, Great Spirit, my Grandfather, forgetting nothing you have made, the stars of the universe and the grasses of the earth." He continued to implore the Great Spirit, Tonkashula, to listen to his prayer to make the earth whole again and his people whole again (especially, I might add, after the devastation of the Wounded Knee massacre, the misery and buffaloless-poverty, living in square, wooden homes on a reservation, and right then in 1931, the blasting and carving of American presidents' faces out of the sacred rock). As the old man continued his supplications to Tonkashula, thin rain clouds gathered and a "scant chill rain" fell from seemingly out of nowhere. Black Elk prayed, "In sorrow I am sending a feeble voice, O Six Powers of the World. Hear me in my sorrow, for I may never call again. O make my people live!"

Indeed, we thought to ourselves as we stood atop the highest point of land east of the Rockies in North America. While the national forests, including this Black Elk Wilderness Area, still remain under the control of the U.S. government, it is not too late for officials to sign a revitalized document representing a final peace to a people. Let their prayer bundles come true. Amid the mystic piping of spring peepers from the lower vales, we said our goodbyes to our fellow climber and wished him well. We made our descent from Black Elk's peak down to the green and rolling prairies and somewhat reluctantly toward our respective homes.

BLACK ELK'S PRAYER ATOP HARNEY PEAK

I discovered this hitherto unpublished prayer among John G. Neihardt's papers (and not included in his *Black Elk Speaks*, 1932) in the W.W. Thompson Folklore Collection at the New York State Historical Association in Cooperstown. I quote from John G. Neihardt: "Black Elk's words, spoken in Sioux, as translated by his son (Ben), taken in shorthand by John Neihardt's daughter, and finally reported by the poet himself…. (It was) Spoken atop a high hill (Harney Peak) in the emptiness of the great plains, (where Nicholas Black Elk) faced west, the power that makes life and that destroys.

>   Grandfather, great mysterious one. You have been always, and before you nothing has been. There is nothing to pray to but you. The star nations all over the universe are yours, and yours are the grasses of the earth. Day in and day out you are the life of things. You are older than all need, older than all pain and prayer.
>   Grandfather, all over the world the faces of living ones are alike. In tenderness they have come up out of the ground. Look upon your children with children in their arms that they may face the winds and walk the good road to the day of quiet.
>   Teach me to walk the soft earth a relative to all that live. Sweeten my heart and fill me with light. Give me the strength to understand and the eyes to see. Help me for without you I am nothing.
>   (1931).

A SELECTIVE LIST OF FORMATIVE MOUNTAIN AND NATURE BOOKS

Barcott, Bruce. *The Measure of a Mountain: Beauty and Terror on Mount Rainier*. Seattle: Sasquatch Books, 1997.

Bird, Isabella. *A Lady's Life in the Rocky Mountains*. New York: Putnam's Sons, 1879.

Douglas, William O. *Of Men and Mountains*. New York: Harper and Row, 1950.

Evans-Wentz, W.Y. *Cuchama and Sacred Mountains*. Athens: Swallow Press/University of Ohio Press, 1981.

Fergusson, Erna. *Dancing Gods: Indian Ceremonials of New Mexico and Arizona*. Albuquerque, 1931.

Fletcher, Colin. *A Thousand Mile Summer*. Berkeley, Cal.: Howell-North Books, 1964.

Frick, Thomas. *The Sacred Theory of Earth*. Berkeley, Cal.: North Atlantic Books, 1986.

Graham, Stephen. *Tramping with a Poet in the Rockies*. New York: Appleton and Company, 1922.

Kent, Rockwell. *Wilderness: A Journal of Quiet Adventure in Alaska*. New York: Modern Library, 1920.

Knighton, José. *Canyon Country's La Sal Mountains: Hiking and Nature Handbook*. Moab: Canyon Country Publications, 1995.

Krakauer, Jon. *Eiger Dreams: Ventures Among Men and Mountains*. New York: Bantam Doubleday, 1997.

McPhee, John. *Rising from the Plains*. New York: Farrar, Straus and Giroux, 1987.

Mills, Enos. *A Rocky Mountain Wonderland*. Boston: Houghton Mifflin, 1915.

Mitchell, Finis. *Wind River Trails: A Hiking and Fishing Guide*. Salt Lake City: Wasatch Publishers, 1975.

Momaday, N. Scott. *The Way to Rainy Mountain*. Albuquerque: University of New Mexico Press, 1968.

Muir, John. *Mountaineering Essays*, ed. Richard F. Fleck. Salt Lake City: University of Utah Press, 1997.

Neihardt, John G. *Black Elk Speaks*, with an introduction by Vine Deloria, Jr. Lincoln: University of Nebraska Press, 1988.

Norgay, Jamling Tenzing. *Touching My Father's Soul: A Sherpa's Journey to the Top of Everest*. San Francisco: Harper Collins, 2001.

Saner, Reg. *The Four-Cornered Falcon: Essays on the Interior West and the Natural Scene*. New York: Kodansha International, 1994.

Stevenson, Robert Louis. *Travels with a Donkey in the Cevennes*. New York: Charles Scribner's Sons, 1903.

Thoreau, Henry David. *The Maine Woods*, with an introduction by Richard F. Fleck. New York: Harper and Row, 1987.

INDEX

ARTISTS:

Bierstadt, Albert, 49, 50.
Hokusai, Ichiryusai, 34, 38.
O'Keeffe, Georgia, 70.
Van Gogh, Vincent, 44, 139.

AUTHORS, LITERARY:

Abbey, Edward, 135, 138–139, 141.
Bird, Isabella, 7–8, 9, 11.
Black Elk, Nicholas, 149–155, 157.
Fergusson, Erna, 76–77, 78, 80.
Frost, Robert, 54–55.
Kawabata, Yasunari, 36.
McPhee, John, 58.
Mills, Enos, 57.
Momaday, N. Scott, 69.
Muir, John, 9, 11, 40–41, 42, 45, 80.
Ortiz, Simon, 68.
Ross, A.C., 54.
Silko, Leslie M., 67–68.
Thoreau, Henry David, 5, 6, 40, 60–61, 69, 97, 98, 99, 140, 146.
Twain, Mark, 145.
Verne, Jules, 93.
Weeks, Rupert, 56.

AUTHORS, SCIENTIFIC:

Cooper, John D., 54.
Deffreys, John, 58.
Frost, Carol, 54, 57.
King, Philip B., 54.
Powell, John Wesley, 7, 13–23.

CLIMBING COMPANIONS:

Barbee, Robert, 7, 8, 10.
Barbour, Dick, 146.
Boucher, Jonny, 38–40, 82–85, 109–110, 111–113.
Borusheski, John, 151–153.
DeLong, Dick, 8.
Fader, Gordon, 69, 71, 109, 128.
Jewell, Jim, 8.
Mackey, Michael, 110, 137.
Reames, Mark, 45, 46, 55, 56, 60, 63, 65, 66, 67, 70, 72–73, 75, 80, 81, 88–92, 93–95, 109, 120–121.
Rodman, Isaac, 49, 50–51, 97–98.
Schroeder, Fr. George, 44, 47, 48, 49, 50–51.
Sutton, William, 49, 50, 53, 55, 56, 59, 61–62, 63, 64, 67, 70, 73, 80, 81.

Exploring Expeditions:

Hallett Expedition, 30.
Hayden Expedition, 93.
Powell Expedition, 7, 14.

Family Members on the trail:

Fleck, Anne DeLeon (mother), 124–127.
Fleck, Jess (daughter-in-law), 131–133.
Fleck, J. Keene (father), 125–127, 135–136.
Fleck, Maura (wife), 106, 118–119, 129–131, 150–155.
Fleck (Aller), Maureen (daughter), 117–118.
Fleck (Foothorap), Michelle, 35, 74, 130.
Fleck, Mini (dog), 82, 83, 84, 102, 104, 105, 106, 129–131.
Fleck, Rich (son), 65–66, 93–95, 117–118, 129–130, 131–133.

Glaciers:

Arapaho Glacier (Colorado), 44.
Paradise Glacier (Washington), 30.
Rowe Glacier (Colorado), 28–30.
Saint Mary's Glacier (Colorado), 47.

Historical Figures:

Byers, William, 14, 19, 21, 22.
Garmon, Samuel, 14, 16, 23.
Keplinger, Lewis, 14, 18, 19, 20, 21, 22, 23.
Long, Maj. Stephen H., 7.
Mountain Jim, 8, 11.

Indian Treaties:

Brunot Treaty, 3.
Fort Laramie Treaty, 145, 154.

Indian Tribes:

Arapaho, 8.
Hopi, 67, 75.
Lakota, 149, 153.
Penobscot, 6.
Shoshone, 56.
Ute, 3, 7, 53, 55–56.

Legends:

Shavano, 1–2.

Legislation:

Wilderness Act of 1964, 79.

Mountain Ranges:

Black Hills (South Dakota), 149–155.
Front Range (Colorado), 54, 55.
La Sal (Utah), 135–143.
Medicine Bow (Wyoming), 21.
Mosquito (Colorado), 115–124.
Mummy (Colorado), 18, 25–32.
Never Summer (Colorado), 11, 22, 29.
Pecos (Colorado), 87–92.
San Francisco Peaks (Arizona), 67, 74, 78.

Index 163

San Juan (Colorado), 93–95.
Sangre de Cristo (Colorado), 2, 66, 67.
Sawatch (Colorado), 1–4.
Uinta (Utah), 53–54.

MUSICIANS:

Scarlatti, Domenico, 83.
Schoenberg, Arnold, 30.

NATIONAL PARK:

Rocky Mountain, 2, 26, 28, 53, 57, 125, 127, 142.

NATURAL PHENOMENA:

Brocken Specter, 11, 37.
Lawn Lake Flood Disaster, 29.
Northern Lights, 5, 8, 10.

PEAKS & SUMMITS:

Agassiz (Arizona), 80.
Antero (Colorado), 1.
Bierstadt (Colorado), 49–52.
Bross (Colorado), 122–123.
Cameron (Colorado), 118–120.
Chapin (Colorado), 25–28.
Chiefs Head (Colorado), 18, 20, 22, 31.
Democrat (Colorado), 117–118.
Elbert (Colorado), 65–66.
Flattop (Colorado), 12, 13.
Fuji (Japan), 11, 29, 33–38.
Grandmother Spider (Taylor Peaks, New Mexico), 67–69, 85.
Grays (Colorado), 43–46.
Hagues (Colorado), 28–31.
Halla San (Korea), 34, 38–40.
Harney (South Dakota), 149–155.
Humphreys (Arizona), 75.
Ida (Colorado), 7.
Jicarita (New Mexico), 90–91.
Katahdin (Maine), 5–7.
Kings (Utah), 57, 59, 60, 61–64.
Laramie (Wyoming), 146–149.
Lincoln (Colorado), 120–122.
Longs (Colorado), 5–23.
McHenry's (Colorado), 17, 18, 19, 22, 23, 31.
Meeker (Colorado), 9, 12, 13.
Monadnock (New Hampshire), 97–99.
Mummy (Colorado), 29, 31.
Pikes (Colorado), 22, 131–133.
Powell (Colorado), 17.
Princeton (Colorado), 1, 108–113.
Quandary (Colorado), 120–122.
Roberts (Alaska), 40–42.
Shavano (Colorado), 1, 3.
Sherman (Colorado), 116–117.
Sneffels (Colorado), 93–95.
Specimen (Colorado), 7, 12.
Torreys (Colorado), 46–48.
Wheeler (New Mexico), 81–85.

RIVERS & LAKES:

Big Thompson River (Colorado), 25.
Colorado River, 7, 14.
Grand Lake (Colorado), 13, 21.

Green River (Utah), 7.
Moosehead Lake (Maine), 5, 6.
Saint Lawrence River (Canada), 6.

Towns:

Estes Park, Colorado, 22, 26.
Grand Lake Village, Colorado, 12.
Green River, Wyoming, 14, 23.
Vernal, Utah, 55.

ABOUT THE AUTHOR

Richard F. Fleck is a retired dean of arts and humanities at the Community College of Denver and now teaches several classes for the University of Northern Colorado at Lowry. He also serves as a graduate advisor for the Master of Arts Program at Prescott College, Arizona. Fleck was full professor of English at the University of Wyoming, where he taught Native American literature and regional literature of the American West before coming to Denver as a dean. In addition to his two novels, *Clearing of the Mist* and *Spirit Mound*, he has published four small-press collections of poems, a scholarly study on Henry David Thoreau and John Muir, and the well-received *Critical Perspectives on Native American Fiction*. He edited *A Colorado River Reader*, which served as the discussion book in seven western states for "Moving Waters," a program funded by the National Endowment for the Humanities. He holds a B.A. from Rutgers University, an M.A. from Colorado State University, and a Ph.D from the University of New Mexico. He and his wife Maura and three children have lived in Ireland and Japan while on research and teaching assignments. He has five grandchildren, Patrick, Catherine, Clare, Ross, and Greta, and another two on the way.

A CHRONOLOGICAL LIST OF BOOKS BY RICHARD F. FLECK

PALMS, PEAKS AND PRAIRIES (poetry), Francestown, NH: The Golden Quill Press, 1967

THE INDIANS OF THOREAU: selections from the Indian Notebooks, ed. Richard F. Fleck. Albuquerque, NM: Hummingbird Press, 1974

COTTONWOOD MOON (poetry). Laramie, WY: Jelm Mountain Press, 1979

CLEARING OF THE MIST, 1st edition (novel). Paradise, CA; Dustbooks, 1979 and 2nd edition published 21 years later: New York: Domhan Books, 2000

OUR NATIONAL PARKS by John Muir and introduced by Richard F. Fleck. Madison: University of Wisconsin Press, 1981

BAMBOO IN THE SUN (poetry). Kobe, Japan: SU Press, 1983

HENRY THOREAU AND JOHN MUIR AMONG THE INDIANS (critical study). Hamden, CT: Archon Books, 1985

THE MAINE WOODS by Henry David Thoreau, introduced by Richard F. Fleck. New York: Harper Perennial Classic, 1987

EARTHEN WAYFARER (poetry). Iowa City, IA: Writers House Press, 1988 (4th book of poems)

ALASKA DAYS WITH JOHN MUIR by Samuel Hall Young, introduced by Richard F. Fleck. Salt Lake City: Peregrine Smith Books, 1991

CRITICAL PERSPECTIVES ON NATIVE AMERICAN FICTION, ed. Richard F. Fleck. Washington, D.C.: Three Continents Press, 1993

WHERE LAND IS MOSTLY SKY (essays). Pueblo, CO: Passeggiata Press, 1997

MOUNTAINEERING ESSAYS by John Muir, edited and introduced by Richard F. Fleck. Salt Lake City: University of Utah Press, 1997 and translated into Korean 7 years later. Seoul, Korea: Jeong Sang Mountain Books, 2004

A COLORADO RIVER READER, ed. Richard F. Fleck. Salt Lake City: University of Utah Press, 2000